SOFT POWER IN FOREIGN POLICY

China's Strategic Use of Trade, Culture, and Diplomacy

SOFT POWER IN FOREIGN POLICY

China's Strategic Use of Trade, Culture, and Diplomacy

Madhura Arekar

Indian Council of Social Science Research

PENTAGON PRESS LLP

First published in 2025

Published by
Indian Council of Social Science Research
(Ministry of Education), Government of India,
Aruna Asaf Ali Marg, New Delhi – 110067.
Phone: 9220521105
Email: prsdivision@icssr.org • Website: www.icssr.org

In association with
PENTAGON PRESS LLP
206, Peacock Lane, Shahpur Jat
New Delhi-110049, India
Contact: 011-26490600

Typeset in AGaramond, 11.5 Point
Printed at Aegean Offset Printers, Greater Noida

ISBN 978-81-991162-9-0

www.pentagonpress.in

Contents

Preface

In today's interconnected world, the exercise of power has evolved far beyond the battlefield. Influence is now built not only through military might or economic pressure, but also through subtle forms of persuasion—through ideas, culture, education, language, and shared values. This transformative approach, known as 'soft power,' is redefining how nations compete and collaborate on the global stage.

This book, *Soft Power in Foreign Policy: China's Strategic Use of Trade, Culture, and Diplomacy*, is based on my doctoral research submitted to the University of Mumbai. It examines how China, often perceived as a hard power giant, has simultaneously developed a sophisticated soft power strategy to secure its position as a global leader. By deploying trade, investment, cultural diplomacy, and language as instruments of influence, China has expanded its footprint not just across borders, but into the minds and societies of other nations.

While the foundation of this book lies in academic inquiry, it has been adapted to reach a broader audience—scholars, diplomats, students, policymakers, and all those interested in the nuances of global politics. The chapters are structured to analyse how each component—trade, investment, culture, and language—functions as a vehicle of China's soft power. Throughout, the central question remains: How does China balance its economic ambitions with cultural appeal to shape the international order?

This intellectual journey was made possible through the mentorship of Professor Dr. Uttara Sahasrabuddhe, whose guidance and insight were instrumental in shaping the research and refining its focus. Her support helped transform this study into something that, I hope, makes a meaningful contribution to the understanding of international relations in the 21st century.

In an era where the battle for global influence is being fought not only through force but also through finesse, this book aims to decode one of the most important and carefully crafted strategies of our time.

Pune
July 2025

Madhura Arekar

Acknowledgements

I express my deepest gratitude to those who made this research and publication possible.

First and foremost, I am profoundly thankful to my research guide, Professor Dr. Uttara Sahasrabuddhe, whose unwavering support, intellectual mentorship, and critical insights provided the foundation for this work. Her encouragement and academic guidance made the entire journey not only possible but truly fulfilling.

My sincere thanks also go to the esteemed faculty of the Department of Civics and Politics, University of Mumbai, for creating a rich and supportive academic environment.

I extend special appreciation to Professor. Dr. Vaibhavi Palsule, Head of the Department of Political Science at Ramnarain Ruia Autonomous College, Matunga, Mumbai for her constant moral support and encouragement during the more challenging phases of this research.

I would like to convey deep gratitude to Professor. Dr. Sanjyot Apte, Head, Department of Political Science, Sir Parashurambhau College, (Autonomous), Pune for her continuous support for my research.

I want to thank the office and library staff at the University of Mumbai's Department of Civics and Politics, as well as the librarians of Jawaharlal Nehru Library (Mumbai University), Dr. P.D. Meghani Library (Ruia College), and the British Council Library (Pune) for their cooperation and for granting access to essential resources and documents.

Finally, I owe my heartfelt gratitude to my family, friends, and well-wishers whose patience, belief, and emotional support allowed me to stay focused and resilient throughout this endeavour.

This book is dedicated to all those who believe in the power of ideas to shape the world.

Madhura Arekar

Chapter One

Introduction

Each country's foreign policy has its own goals to achieve. The promotion of national interest is one of the important objectives of foreign policy.

The current world system is multi-polar. It is dominated by ever increasing economic interdependence. Nation-states also face challenges from non-traditional security issues like terrorism and climate change. Nation-states need to achieve national interest in the context of economic interdependence. It has been observed that to realise foreign policy objectives, countries should strengthen themselves in respect of military, economy, and human and material resources. If they expand their capability, they could exercise national power. For scholars of international relations national power implies possession of resources that transforms into influence. The history of International Relations is full of such examples where powerful nations had changed the behaviour of less powerful nations.

To get the desired effect of national power it should be implemented as a combination of hard and soft facets. Foreign policy should reflect the balance between hard and soft power. Hard power means the use of military, economic sanctions to compel a nation-state. Soft power means to influence other countries by using culture, values, and language. Hard power alone will not work in international relations; it must be supplemented by soft power.

'Joseph Nye is the first person who introduced the concept of soft power'.[1] He used the term 'soft power' for the first time in the 1990s when the Cold War was in its last phase. The USSR was on the verge of decline. For a short period, the world system became unipolar with the USA as the only superpower. Soon after, the uni-polar world turned into a multi-polar world. At that time Nye realised the need for soft power to be used by America. During the Cold War, both the superpowers used to employ hard and soft power. It was a different situation. In a multi-polar world, America faced the challenge from Asia-Pacific countries. Then onwards soft power has been the issue of discussion in the field of International Relations.

The 21st century has seen the rise of China as the biggest economy in the world. China's foreign policy has experienced drastic changes after the death of Mao. The People's Republic of China attained independence in 1949. Mao Zedong became its first president. Under his leadership, the foreign policy of China exported the socialist revolution. In 1978, China had adopted market reforms. President Deng Xiaoping has been credited for this initiative. Due to its economic reforms, China opened up its economy to the rest of the world. Deng's successor, Jiang Zemin, continued with the same policy. Under the leadership of Hu Jintao, China's foreign policy promoted principles like Peaceful Development and Harmonious World. Xi Jinping carried out some bold foreign policy initiatives in the form of the Belt and Road Initiative (BRI) and Asian Infrastructure Investment Bank (AIIB). Chinese foreign policy is a reflection of its domestic policies. These leaders aimed at Chinese domestic development. They came up with their own ideas to deal with China's domestic issues like corruption, lack of social security measures, and improving the standard of living.

The Chinese government has recognised the importance of soft power and initiated various policies in that direction. It includes the establishment of Confucius institutions abroad to spread Chinese culture and language. China has arranged high-profile events like the Beijing Olympics and the Shanghai Expo to introduce Chinese values to the world. China has increased trade and investments in Africa, Latin America and Southeast

Asia. China is a newcomer in the field of soft power. European countries and America are masters in this sphere. One can also try to create the Chinese notion of soft power and apply that notion in assessing the effectiveness of Chinese soft power. This book is a study of the use of soft power by China.

Literature

China is a popular subject of study; hence several scholars have studied and published books and articles on different aspects of the foreign policy of China.

Jonathan Fenby, in his work, *The Penguin History of Modern China: The Fall and Rise of a Great Power, 1850 to the Present*'[2] has examined how China became a great power in the late twentieth century. This book is an excellent account on the history of modern China. It covers the period from the 19th to the 21st century. It describes the phase of upheaval and stability experienced by the Chinese people. It not only observes their leaders' contribution in the development of Chinese polity, society and economy but also assesses the impact of their policy programmes on China. It has been argued that Chinese history is unique. In the age of globalisation, China is going through a multiplicity of challenges. Though it is the world's second largest economy, it is facing various problems like lack of social security measures, absence of democracy at the party level, bureaucratic capitalism, and rise in corruption.

Manoranjan Mohanty's book, *Ideology Matters: China from Mao Zedong to Xi Jinping*'[3] reviews the evolution of Communist ideology in China. From 1949 to 2016 China has been ruled by five generations of leaders. Each leader and his ideology have influenced China's domestic and foreign policies. This book is an elaborate account of these ideologies and their impact on China's polity, economy, and society. It describes the contribution of Mao's thoughts in bringing about socialism in China. It discusses Deng Xiaoping's theory of building socialism with Chinese characteristics. Under the leadership of Jiang Zemin, China went in for three important developments. Hu Jintao advocated the idea of peaceful development. Xi

Jinping figured out the aim of the Chinese Dream. All this has been extensively written in this book.

China's concepts of development and national interest are rooted in Chinese philosophy. There are some useful books that throw light on this link.

Karyn L. Lai's *An Introduction to Chinese Philosophy*' is one such.[4] This book is a systematic account of Chinese philosophy. At the outset, it explains the features of Chinese philosophy. In the subsequent chapters it examines Chinese philosophical traditions like Confucianism, Mohism, Daoism, and Legalism. The chapter on Confucianism focuses on the concepts of 'Ren' and 'Li'. In Mohism, the author points out the Mohist ideas of maximising collective good. The philosophy of Daoism reflects upon the meaning of the word 'Dao' that is 'path' or 'way'. The text on Legalism states three basic themes. They are penal code, technique, and power. The chapter on Chinese Buddhism has been divided into two parts—Indian Buddhism and Chinese Buddhism. In all the chapters, the author has included opinions of scholars on Chinese philosophy. He has also incorporated debatable issues in each philosophy.

JeeLoo Liu Has written *An introduction to Chinese philosophy: From ancient philosophy to Chinese Buddhism.*"[5] This book covers ancient Chinese philosophy and Chinese Buddhism. In the beginning, the author explains features of Chinese philosophy. The second chapter elaborates on Confucianism. It examines two key elements of Confucius philosophy. They are 'Zhong' and 'Shu'; the former means 'loyalty' and the latter 'empathy'. The author has discussed the base of Confucius philosophy which implies building a moral or social hierarchical structure. He has tried to study 'loyalty' and 'empathy' in the context of this structure. It is pointed out that Confucius had created moral structure of society. It includes the emperor at the top, ministers at the middle and people at bottom. Here, everybody is in relation to one another. The individual plays the role in accordance with relations. While performing respective duties, everybody is obliged to follow the virtue of loyalty. Another key principle of Confucius philosophy is 'shu', meaning to treat individuals in a good way. The author has also described Confucius's ideas on politics.

Here, it is stated that the ruler should take care of the moral development of the individual. If the ruler behaves morally, then individuals will obey him willingly. It concludes that the Confucius person is true in all fields of life. The entire book is a remarkable work on Chinese philosophy.

Chan, Wing. Tsit's book, *A Source Book in Chinese Philosophy*[6] has described the evolution of Chinese philosophy in the ancient, medieval, and modern periods. It has explained Chinese philosophical trends like Confucianism, Taoism, and Buddhism. With the help of this book, one can examine the influence of Chinese philosophy on Chinese society. This book is also helpful in conducting a comparative analysis of Chinese and Western philosophy.

Some books have elaborated on the economic transition of China.

G.C. Chow's *China's Economic Transformation*[7], provides a systematic account on the development of the Chinese economy. It has described the evolution of Chinese economy from ancient to modern times. It has discussed China's economic growth with the help of statistics. It has analysed individual sectors like banking and the financial system, trade, investment corporations, and insurance companies. The author has argued that a state-controlled economy has impeded the growth of the private sector in China. It has also raised the issue of prevalent corruption in economic reforms.

John Gitting's *The Changing Face of China: from Mao to Market*[8] book describes the changes in Chinese political, social, and economic life from 1949 to 2006. It covers Mao's programmes of Great Leap Forward and Cultural Revolution. It examines leadership transformation from Mao to Deng Xiaoping. It explains the nature of the economic reforms introduced by Deng Xiaoping. It also elaborates change in foreign policy agenda after the death of Mao. This book gives us detailed analytical and factual information about how today's China has evolved.

Joseph, William A. in his *Politics in China: An Introduction*'[9] gives an excellent account of the development of China's economy from 1978. It highlights the bottom-up approach in China's economic reforms. It focuses on the changes in agriculture, rural enterprises, state-owned companies, and urban reforms. It illustrates the progress of the Chinese economy.

W.H. Overholt's *The Rise of China*[10] is a comprehensive account of China's economic development since 1978. The author has appreciated China's efforts in transforming the economy. He is optimistic about China's progress. He has also recognised the importance of the U.S.-China relationship.

Ezra F. Vogel, in his work, *Deng Xiaoping and the Transformation of China*[11] has highlighted the contribution of Deng Xiaoping in the transformation of the Chinese economy. The book describes the gradual way in which Deng Xiaoping has introduced economic reforms in China. It also touches upon his political life. It provides a comprehensive understanding of Chinese economic reforms.

Some works are useful in understanding contemporary Chinese foreign policy.

Howard W. French's *China's Second Continent: How a million migrants are building a new empire in Africa*[12] examines China's involvement in Africa through investment and trade. It has been observed that there is a significant increase in China's involvement in Africa. Hence, Africa has become a 'second continent' of China. It is stated that some people in Africa welcome China and some feel that it is new colonisation. According to the author, there is a link between Western colonisation and China's engagement with Africa. European countries did compete with each other to become powerful. Similarly, China is competing with America and wants to be a global power. China with its investment and trade is enhancing influence in Africa.

Martin Jacques's *When China Rules the World*[13] argues that China will make a new world order on its own terms and conditions. It points to the Chinese assertion to dominate the world. It elucidates the picture of domestic level of China as well as its position at the international level. It has been suggested that in future Western values, their culture, and institutions will not be dominant. The increasing sphere of influence of China is explained in the book.

Marc Lanteigne's *Chinese Foreign Policy: An introduction*[14] examines the expansion of China's foreign policy in the context of the rapidly altering international system. Its first chapter gives information in detail about institutions that form Chinese foreign policy. The second chapter explains China's economic growth in the era of globalisation. The third chapter is on China's participation in various international and regional organisations. The fifth chapter deals with China-USA relations. The sixth chapter is on China's relations with Asia-Pacific countries and the seventh chapter is about general Chinese diplomacy.

Liu, Binjie Lie has authored *China's Philosophy on Foreign Affairs in the 21st Century.*[15] This book states that Chinese foreign policy is for maintaining world peace and encouraging common development to create a harmonious world. It has been held that China will never pose a threat to the world. It explains four key principles of Confucius philosophy which have been reflected in recent Chinese foreign policy. These four principles are righteousness, benevolence, forbearance, and harmony. This book analyses the philosophical base of Chinese foreign policy.

The notion of soft power was developed primarily by Joseph Nye. He propounded the concept of Soft Power in 1990.

Joseph S. Nye Jr.'s *Soft Power*[16] is explained in an article on the change in the nature of international politics after the disintegration of the Soviet Union. It has discussed how the USA still holds the status of a superpower in international relations. At the same time, it has suggested that the USA should understand the altering power equations in international relations. It has been argued that in a multi-polar world no country can rely only on hard power to achieve desired results. A country should use its policies and culture to influence other countries to get the desired result. In other words, a country should use soft power. This article elucidates the significance of soft power.

Nye has further modified the concept in a more recent article.

Joseph S. Nye's article '*Get Smart: Combining Hard and Soft Power*'[17] has emphasised smart power which implies a smart combination of hard and soft power tools. The author opines that a country should not over-emphasise either hard or soft power. It should go for a smart combination of both. To combine the sources of hard and soft power needs Contextual

Intelligence. Contextual Intelligence means the ability of policy-makers to understand the context. Contextual Intelligence helps to create smart power. The author has explained this concept by giving examples of some U.S. presidents. This article was written in the context of the Iraq war. Hence, the author has suggested that America should utilise smart power to strengthen its credibility in the Muslim world.

Nye's *Soft Power: The Means to Success in World Politics*[18] has provided a detailed account of the term 'Soft Power'. He has described a context of current International Relations which compels us to ponder upon the changing nature of power. He has examined the concept of soft power and its sources like culture, political values, and foreign policy. His illustration of soft power mainly centred on American experience. In addition, he has elaborated the role of public diplomacy in creating soft power. He has also pointed out the limitations of soft power resources. This book has indeed contributed to the development of the concept of soft power.

There are many books and articles that analyse the impact and importance of the use of various instruments of Chinese soft power.

Shaun Breslin, in an article titled *The Soft Notion of China's 'Soft Power'*[19] states that there is no common definition of soft power. It changes in accordance with the observer's perspective. The scope of soft power covers economic aspects and other hard resources. It comments on the Chinese scholars' opinion on Chinese soft power. For them soft power is to create a positive image of China. In this context, the author has explained an inclusive definition of Chinese soft power. According to him, it involves national image promotion, normative power promotion, and imagined power. It is argued that developing countries are attracted towards Chinese soft power. The author has highlighted the complexity involved in the concept of soft power in general. He has pointed out that there is blurred line between hard and soft factors of soft power.

Bates Gill and Yanzhong Huang have written *Sources and limits of Chinese 'soft power'*.[20] It examines three sources of China's soft power. They are culture, domestic values and policies and foreign policy. Its cultural segment indicates an increase in the number of foreigners learning

Mandarin with the help of statistical data. At the same time it points out the negative impact of expanding Chinese culture on the USA's cultural resource. The domestic values and policies evaluate a positive result of Chinese economic reforms in the form of improvement in lifestyles and tourism activity in China. It also reflects on the appreciation of the Beijing consensus by Southeastern, Latin American and African countries. The nature of foreign policy mentions China's policy of co-operation with neighbours, its efforts to resolve disputes, its membership in international organisations and its interest in regional multilateral relations. It has tried to discover China's effectiveness in exercising soft power by giving statistics about the popularity of Chinese sources in different countries like India, Africa, Latin America, and Western countries.

Yanzhong Huang and Sheng Ding's article titled *Dragon's underbelly: An analysis of China's soft power*[21] tries to assess China's soft power. It studies China's soft power resources and its capability to use them to achieve the desired results. The authors have maintained that China has attained magnificent rewards in the field of soft power resources and utilised those resources to get the desired outcomes. This has led to the decrease in U.S. influence at the global level. However, they have asserted that China has not yet developed a perfect mix of soft power resources. If one compares China with the USA, it is evident that the Chinese culture and development model is lagging behind. Further, it is stated that China's use of soft power resources is confined to Southeast Asia. It has impressed African and Latin American countries. Still there exists the threat of a China theory in Western countries. The authors believe that there are some causes restraining China's soft power capability. Firstly, it cannot use soft power resources like culture or domestic values in the fullest sense due to the closed political system. Secondly, there are limited soft power resources. Hence it is argued that China's soft power capability remains vulnerable.

Joshua Kurlantzick's *Charm offensive: How China's soft power is transforming the world*[22] examined various soft power tools employed by China. It discusses the evolution of soft power policy of China. It has contextualised the term 'A Charm Strategy.' It elaborates culture and business as instruments of China's soft power.

The Mingjiang Li. edited book, *Soft Power: China's Emerging Strategy in International Politics*[23] offers a comprehensive study of China's soft power. It is divided into four parts. The first part focuses on a discourse on China's soft power in China and abroad. The second part discusses China's soft power strategy which includes sources like education and culture. The third part examines China's relations with countries like Australia and Africa in the context of its robust efforts to promote soft power. The last part summarises various observations made in earlier segments.

In *China's Soft Power Deficit*[24] Nye opined that China has realised the significance of soft power which can be seen through various policies like Chinese economic assistance to African and Latin American countries, dissemination of Chinese culture and language and arranging high-profile events like the Shanghai Expo. The author has considered that the suppression of civil society and human rights violations by the Chinese government are creating obstacles in the successful implementation of Chinese soft power measures. He has suggested that China should improve its politics to use soft power resources successfully.

Parama S. Palit has written *Analysing China's Soft Power Strategy and Comparative Indian Initiatives.*[25] The book provides a comprehensive understanding of China's soft power in South Asia and Southeast Asia, Africa, Latin America, and Central Asia. It touches upon different tools of Chinese soft power and their effectiveness across these continents. It discusses Indian soft power strategies. It incorporates the comparative analysis of the impact of soft power of China and India.

David Shambaugh's *Power Shift China and Asia's New Dynamics*[26] examines the rise of China and its impact on the Asian order. It describes China's increasing sphere of influence and inevitability of China in regional economic growth. It also focuses on China's active diplomacy. It helps in understanding contemporary Asian politics.

There are several books and articles on China's Belt and Road Initiative.

Michael Clarke has written *The Belt and Road Initiative: China's New Grand Strategy?*[27] According to the author, the BRI is perceived in three different ways—first, to counter the USA in the Asia-Pacific region and restrain the rise of China. Second, it would give economic benefits to China and reduce the gap between the eastern and western regions of China. It would channelise the excessive production capacity. Third, the BRI can create a soft power narrative. He has argued that the BRI aims to promote China's domestic economic interests.

Romi Jain in an article titled '*China's Economic Expansion in South Asia: Strengths, Challenges, and Opportunities*"[28] argued that despite controversies associated with BRI projects, South Asian countries are accepting China's economic engagement. The author further stated the causes for such a welcoming approach by those countries. Firstly, they are fearful of India which surpasses them with huge territory and population. So, they want China to prevent India's possible hegemonic tendencies. Secondly, they lack infrastructure and China is ready to pour money for its development.

S. Kondapalli and H. Xiaowen have edited a book titled *One Belt One Road: China's Global Outreach*.[29] It deals with China's novel Belt and Road Initiative (BRI). It provides the information on several projects covered under the Initiative. Contributors have touched upon different dimensions of the BRI such as its political economy, China's need for energy, BRI's portrayal in media, its maritime angle, and its geostrategic aspect. It has also pointed out challenges to the BRI.

Xiao Fang in his article, *The Belt and Road Initiative: Connecting China and Central Europe*[30] has commented on China-Central Europe relations in the context of the BRI and argued that the BRI would foster cooperation with Central Europe. There already exists a 16+1 mechanism which promotes people-to-people exchanges and high-level meetings between China and Central European countries. The author has argued that Central European countries are emerging economies. Hence, they would gain benefits under the BRI, particularly in the field of financing facilities.

Hong Yu in an article titled *China's Belt and Road Initiative and its Implications for Southeast Asia*[31] has stated that China percieves Southeast Asia as a key element of the BRI especially for its maritime component. The author has pointed out a division on BRI amongst Southeast Asian countries. Countries like Cambodia and Laos are optimistic about it whereas Indonesia, Vietnam, Malaysia, and the Philipines are looking at it with caution. They are worried about overdependence on China and the emergence of a Sino-centric order in Southeast Asia.

The concept of soft power has gained significance since its introduction in the study of international relations theoretically as well as practically. In this field, China's soft power has received much attention considering its fast-growing economy. Researchers, academicians, and policymakers in China and in other parts of the world have tried to evaluate China's soft power policy. They have advanced different arguments in respect of Chinese soft power. It often becomes just a description of Chinese soft power policies. Many scholars have focussed on the cultural aspect of Chinese soft power. They look at it as a reaction to Chinese threat theory.

However, most of these works have not particularly looked at the Chinese notion of soft power. This particular book will attempt to understand the Chinese notion of soft power whose roots China traces back to ancient Chinese philosophy. It attempts:

- To create the Chinese concept of soft power and try to understand its roots in ancient Chinese philosophy.
- To assess the instruments of Chinese soft power and illustrate their contribution in making China a global power with examples.
- To examine the impact of Chinese soft power instruments on various regions.
- To analyse China's soft power policy in the context of its domestic policies.
- To point out the limits of Chinese soft power policy.

Hypothesis

China has evolved its own concept of soft power. It employs soft power instruments to create a convergence of its own national interest and that of others.

Research Questions

This research aims to seek answers to the following questions:

1. What is the meaning of soft power?
2. What is the Chinese understanding of soft power and what are its instruments?
3. In what way does China use trade, investment, and culture and language to construct the convergence of its national interests with that of other countries?

This book uses historical and analytical methods of research. The research uses primary source like official papers. It also incorporates secondary data like articles and books.

This research focuses on China's soft power policy. It focuses on China's understanding of the concept of soft power. It deals with China's trade relations with different countries. It describes the influence of Chinese culture and language on various countries.

It is also important to note some of the important limitations of this research. One such limitation is that the research does not use sources in Chinese language. It is based on both primary and secondary data only in English. Further, it does not include the period of monarchy in China, nor does it deal with analysis of the Chinese political system and its domestic politics. It also does not compare China's soft power policy with that of other countries.

The Chapters

Chapter One: Introduction

It provides the framework of the research area. It gives the significance of the study of foreign policy. It states the inevitability of hard and soft power in a country's foreign policy making. It explains why scholars are fascinated by the phenomena of Chinese soft power.

This chapter includes a literature survey. It incorporates primary and secondary sources such as government documents from official websites and books and articles. The scope of the literature review is diverse. There are books and articles on Chinese economy, soft power, and Chinese soft power.

It describes the justification of this particular research. Though academicians and practitioners have worked on Chinese soft power, their study often becomes descriptive in nature like understanding Chinese soft power policies and emphasising on culture as an instrument of China's soft power. This research is an attempt to create the Chinese notion of soft power and assess its different instruments.

Chatper Two: Meaning and instruments of soft power

This chapter presents the evolution and meaning of the concept of soft power. It gives a detailed account of the instruments of soft power and scrutinises the importance of soft power in foreign policy. Besides, this chapter illuminates China's contribution in the progress of the concept of soft power with the help of constructivism and realism. It attempts to discover the Chinese notion of soft power with the help of Chinese philosophy.

It discusses Joseph Nye's contribution in the field of soft power. In his article titled 'Changing Nature of World Power' he has pointed out that, factors such as technology, education and economic growth are becoming more important in the current era. He has underlined the fact that soft power is an attractive power. It is not the same as influence because influence can be created with economic sanctions or threats. Though persuasion is a part of it, soft power is not just about persuasion.

He has further identified resources of soft power.

- **Culture**

  I. High Culture—Literature, Art, Education: For example, student exchange programs, Shakespeare, Lord of the Rings, Harry Potter, etc.

  II. Popular Culture—Mass Entertainment: For example, Hollywood movies like Independence Day, National Treasure, etc.

- **Political Values:** Values that government observes at domestic as well as international levels: Democracy, Freedom, Human Rights.
- **Foreign Policy:** For example, Marshall Plan.

He has elaborated the role of public diplomacy in channelising the resources of soft power and explained how America has used it effectively throughout the Cold War.

China is a newcomer in the field of soft power. It is pertinent here to reflect upon some aspects of Chinese philosophy and their applicability in the Chinese concept of soft power. In Chinese philosophy, ethics are discussed in the context of its practical applications. Chinese philosophers pay less attention to universal or normative standards and principles. For example, China provides aid to countries without terms and conditions. There is the principle of self-cultivation in Chinese philosophy which implies that only a cultivated man can legitimately lead the world. For example, the Belt and Road Initiative can be analyzed as China's efforts to cultivate itself and to legitimately lead the world.

Chapter Three: Trade as an Instrument of Soft Power

This chapter estimates the role of trade as an instrument of Chinese soft power to construct the convergence of national interest. It elaborates Chinese trade relations with Asian countries.

It also examines the evolution of the Chinese economy since 1978. The development of the Chinese economy is an interesting phenomenon to study because such improvement has been exhibited only by small countries like Hong Kong, Singapore, Taiwan, homogenous countries like South Korea and Japan and under-populated countries like Saudi Arabia.

Experts have linked the economic reforms in China with Chinese nationalism. Some have described reforms as socialism with Chinese characteristics.

Chinese economic reforms have contributed to the development of coastal areas. They have put economics above politics. They have loosened the central control over the provinces. Cosmopolitan culture has developed especially in the coastal areas. It has been observed that the economic reforms are the result of co-operation between the Central government and the local people. Shekou in Guangdong is the first place in China where FDI was allowed. China initiated agricultural reforms along with industrial reforms. In fact, agricultural reforms are the result of local peasants' initiative, wherein they decided to farm land as individual families and not as communes. Communes were abolished in 1982.

Reforms also brought changes in state-owned industries, private industries and movement of labour. China's entry into the WTO in 2001 was a landmark in the process of China's economic growth. It has been argued that China's reforms and foreign policy are interlinked. The Go Global and Western Development strategies are examples.

China's domestic economic growth has facilitated its external economic relations. As a result, trade has become a key area of foreign policy. China's bilateral trade has promoted mutual benefits conducive to a peaceful environment. In this context, it can be claimed that China is utilising trade as an instrument of soft power.

This chapter describes China's Free Trade Agreements (FTA) with different countries like the China-ASEAN FTA, China-Pakistan FTA and China-Bangladesh FTA. For China, ASEAN countries offer an abundant natural resource and for ASEAN countries, regional sustainable development was important because till the 1990s it was just a sub-regional organisation. Besides, China's access to the WTO raised concerns from ASEAN countries about Chinese competition in exports and attracting FDI. One can take into consideration the rapid growth in bilateral trade. For example, in 1991 it was less than 8 bn U.S. dollars and in 2006, 160.8 bn U.S. dollars. The China–ASEAN Expo has become a medium in facilitating FTA. Statesmen from ASEAN countries have often expressed the indispensability of China in bilateral economic relations. The China-Pakistan FTA can be useful for strengthening economic relationship between the two countries as their relationship has always been co-operative in nature due to the enmity with India. The China–Bangladesh FTA is still in the process of completion. It indicates a positive response from Bangladesh to further the ties with China.

Chapter Four: Investment as an Instrument of Soft Power

This chapter judges the task of investment as an instrument of Chinese soft power to construct the convergence of national interests with special reference to One Belt One Road (OBOR).

China's economic progress is unstoppable, and investment has played a very important role in it. Two significant initiatives in China's investment policy were the Western Development and Go Global Strategies. China's eastern provinces benefited from economic reforms However, it created a regional disparity between the western and eastern provinces. The Chinese government has initiated the Western Development Strategy to improve the economic conditions of the western regions by building infrastructure projects. But there was an absence of foreign players. In 2000, they launched the 'Go Global' campaign to promote China's overseas investments. The Belt and Road Initiative can be considered a landmark in China's investment policy. It aims to create connectivity by building infrastructure in participant countries.

China's declaration of the 'Silk Road Economic Belt and Maritime Silk Road'[32] policy has become an important point of discussion in China's foreign policy. For some, it is a geo-economic and geo-strategic policy, China's ambitious plan to create a Sino-centric Asian order, and for some it is a win-win policy. Few opined that it is to counter America in the Asia–Pacific region. For some, it would reduce the gap between the eastern and western regions of China. According to some scholars, it would solve the problem of overcapacity in industry. Some experts have argued that the BRI is to enhance the Chinese sphere of influence.

This chapter discusses the BRI projects in countries in Southeast Asia, South Asia, Europe and Central Asia like major projects in Malaysia are the East Coast Rail Link (ECRL), Malaysia-China Kuantan Industrial Park (MCKIP) in Pahang, Malacca Gateway National Maritime Park, and Iskandar Malaysia development in Johor. It will provide the development of Malaysian seaport hinterland and a rail network. It can establish the connectivity between Singapore-Malaysia-Thailand. But the Malaysian government has demanded adjustments in the projects. Sri Lanka is an example of China's debt diplomacy. From the beginning, officials in Sri Lanka were sceptical about Hambantota port. The first major loan Sri Lanka took from China was of $ 307 million. Formally it was opened in 2010, yet ships preferred Colombo Port. It paved the wave for increasing construction cost. Therefore, the Rajapaksa government took a loan from China of $ 757 million. Later, President Maithripala Sirisena decided to scrutinise Sri Lanka's financial deals.

Participating countries have many issues in the implementation of the BRI such as domestic concerns over local unemployment, increasing debt and the fear of China's dominance. But still, they are ready to revise the terms and co-operate with China.

Chapter Five: Culture and Language as Instruments of Soft Power

This chapter evaluates the function of Chinese culture and Chinese language as the instrument of Chinese soft power in constructing the convergence of national interests. It highlights the role of education, Confucius institutions, Chinese Diaspora, and tourism in spreading Chinese culture and language.

Recently released movies like '2012', 'The Martian' and 'The Meg' wherein Chinese scientists are contributing to science and technology have helped in creating a positive image of China. It could be an indicator of the world's changing perspective towards China. China is utilising a combination of high culture and popular culture to extend its influence.

China has established Chinese educational institutions in different parts of the world, and it offers attractive programs and provides scholarships to students to study at Chinese universities. The Ministry of Education of the PRC has started the '*Undergraduate Foundation Program for International Students on the Chinese Government Scholarship Program*'.[33] It promotes the spread of the Chinese language. Recently, China has signed an agreement on mutual recognition of qualifications and academic degrees in higher education with 54 countries. Also, it has set up educational cooperation and exchange with 188 countries and regions and 46 international organisations.[34] Another notable drive carried out by the

Chinese government is the Silk Road, Belt and Road Initiative scholarship that covers Bachelors, Masters and Ph.D. degrees in China.[35]

Currently, there are 541 Confucius Institutions (CI) and 1,170 Confucius classrooms around the world. It has been observed that, CIs are more popular in Asian countries. But Western countries are suspicious about them due to the unpredictability of their intentions and their link with the Chinese government.

The Chinese Diaspora is huge in number; its presence across the continents is trying to build a benign image of China. Campaigns throughout the world to support the Beijing Olympics highlight the role of the Chinese Diaspora. Its contribution is at multiple levels. For instance, to accelerate the Chinese economy, to promote the Chinese language and culture, to create the convergence of interests.

Tourism has started playing a crucial role in Chinese foreign policy very recently. The China National Tourism Administration was looking after tourism, but it was replaced by the 'Ministry of Culture and Tourism of the People's Republic of China'[36] established in 2018. It promotes tourism in China. Besides, there is the 'China Tourism Academy'[37] which was set up in 2008. Tourism helps in shaping China's foreign policy and has the potential to affect international politics.

Chapter Six: Conclusion

This chapter attempts to provide an overall analysis of Chinese soft power. It evaluates China's soft power policy and examines the impact of Chinese soft power instruments.

China's foreign policy has experienced a roller coaster ride since its establishment. During the Cold War, it adhered to the socialist bloc. According to observers, the attitude of Chinese diplomats was very passive at that time. Chinese domestic economic reforms have influenced China's foreign policy to a great extent. Trade and investment have been playing a vital role in foreign policy since 1978. A remarkable moment at the end of the 20th century was the steady rise of China's economic power. Though the incident of Tiananmen Square has acted as a bottleneck in the process, it was not able to reject the necessity of China in the process of regional economic development.

Chinese diplomacy became active. China extended help to Southeast Asian countries during the Asian financial crisis. China got entry into the WTO in 2001. Simultaneously, China's assertion in the South China Sea and its increasing military power has created suspicions about China's rise. Western discourse on China got occupied with the China Threat Theory. Meanwhile, foreign policy experts in China were discussing China's soft power. Chinese President Hu Jintao promoted the concept of China's peaceful development. The Chinese government initiated different avenues to underline a soft image of China such as establishment of CI's, the Olympic Games, and the Chinese Expo.

Experts have claimed that in spite of being new in the field of soft power, China has performed very well in it. The understanding of China's soft power indeed compels one to de-Americanise the notion of soft power. It has been argued that China's domestic policies are linked to China's foreign policy. Hence, it will be an interesting analysis to examine the effectiveness of China's soft power tools in creating the convergence of its national interests and that of others. An interpretation of Chinese philosophical facets like self–cultivation, mandate of heaven and harmony as the foundation of China's soft power notion could provide the alternative narration in the field of soft power in general. In a nutshell, the influence of China's trade policy, the Belt and Road Initiative and its cultural and educational institutions varies from place to place. One also has to consider the context in which soft power tools are implemented.

NOTES

1. Nye Jr, J. S (1990). 'Soft Power.' *Foreign Policy,* 80, pp. 153-171. Retrieved from https://www.jstor.org/stable/1148580, accessed on 17 September 2015.
2. Fenby, J, (2013). *The Penguin History of Modern China: The Fall and Rise of a Great Power, 1850 to the Present.* England: Penguin Books.
3. Mohanty, M. (2014). *Ideology Matters: China From Mao Zedong to Xi Jinping.* Delhi: Aakar Books.
4. Lai, K. L. (2008). *An Introduction to Chinese Philosophy.* New York: Cambridge University Press.

5. Liu, J. L. (2006). *An Introduction to Chinese Philosophy: From Ancient Philosophy to Chinese Buddhism.* UK: Blackwell Publishiong.
6. Chan, W. T. (1963). *A Source Book in Chinese Philosophy.* New Jersey: Princeton University Press.
7. Chow, G. C. (2015). *China's Economic Transformation.* UK: John Wiley and Sons, Incorporated.
8. Gittings, J. (2006). *The Changing Face of China from Mao to Market.* New York: Oxford University Press.
9. Joseph, W. A. (2014). *Politics in China an Introduction.* New York: Oxford University Press.
10. Overholt, W. H. (1993). *The rise of China: How economic reform is creating a new superpower.* New York: WW Norton & Company.
11. Vogel, E. F. (2011). *Deng Xiaoping and the Trasformation of China.* London: The Belknap Press of Harvard University Press.
12. French, H. W. (2014). *China's second continent: How a million migrants are building a new empire in Africa.* New York: Vintage Books.
13. Jacques, M. (2009). *When China rules the world: the end of the Western world and the birth of global order.* New York: The Penguin Press.
14. Lanteigne, M. (2016). *Chinese Foreign Policy: An Introduction.* London and New York: Routledge Taylor and Francis Group.
15. Liu, B. (2006). *China's Philosophy on Foreign Affairs in the 21st Century.* Foreign Language Press.
16. Nye Jr, J. S. op. cit., p. 153.
17. Nye Jr, J. S. (2009). 'Get Smart: Combining Hard and Soft Power.' *Foreign Policy,* 88(4), pp. 160-163. Retrieved from https://www.jstor.org/stable/20699631, accessed on 17 September 2015.
18. Nye Jr, J. S. (2012). *Soft Power: The Means to Success in World Politics.* New Delhi: KW Publishers Pvt. Ltd.
19. Breslin, S. (2011). *The Soft Notion of China's 'Soft Power'.* London: Chatham House. pp. 1-18. Retrieved from https://www.chathamhouse.org/sites/default/files/public/Research/Asia/0211pp_breslin.pdf, accessed on 13 May 2016.
20 Gill, B. & Huang, Y. (2006). 'Sources and limits of Chinese 'Soft Power'. *Survival, 48*(2), pp. 17-36. Retrieved from https://www.comw.org/cmp/fulltext/0606gill.pdf, accessed on 25 March 2016.
21. Huang, Y. & Ding, S. (2006). 'Dragon's underbelly: An analysis of China's soft power.' *East Asia,* 23(4), pp. 22-44. Retrieved from DOI:10.1007/BF03179658, accessed on 25 April 2016.
22. Kurlantzick, J. (2007). *Charm Offensive:How China's Soft Power is Transforming the World.* New Haven: Yale University Press.
23. M, Li. (ed.). (2009). *Soft Power: China's Emerging Strategy in International Politics.* Lexington Books.
24. Nye Jr, J. S. (2012, May 8). 'China's Soft Power Deficit.' *WSJ.* Retrieved from https:/

/www.wsj.com/articles/SB10001424052702304451104577389923098678842 accessed on 25 March 2016.

25. Palit, P. S. (2017). *Analysing China's Soft Power Strategy and Comparative Indian Initiative*. New Delhi: Sage Publications India Pvt. Ltd.
26. Shambaugh, D. (ed.). (2006). *Power Shift: China and Asia's New Dynamics*. Berkeley, Los Angeles, London: University of California Press.
27. Clarke, M. (2017). 'The Belt and Road Initiative: China's New Grand Strategy?' *Asia Policy*, (24), pp. 71-79. Retrieved from https://www.jstor.org/stable/26403204, accessed on 22 September 2020.
28. Jain, R. (2018). 'China's Economic Expansion in South Asia: Strengths, Challenges and Opportunities.' *International Journal of Asian Affairs*, 31 (1/2), pp. 21-36. Retrieved from https://www.jstor.org/stable/26608821, accessed on 20 August 2020.
29. S, Kondapalli & H. Xiaowen (eds.). (2017). *One Belt One Road: China's Global Outreach*. New Delhi: Pentagon Press.
30. Fang, X. (2015). 'The Belt and Road Initiative: Connecting China and Central Europe'. *International Issues and Slovac Foreign Policy Affairs*, 24(3), pp. 3-14. Retrieved from https://www.jstor.org/stable/26591865?seq=11#metadata_info_tab_contents, accessed on 1 August 2020.
31. Yu, H. (2017). 'China's Belt and Road Initiative and its Implications for Southeast Asia.' *Asia Policy*, (24), pp. 117-122. Retrieved from https://www.jstor.org/stable/26403210, accessed on 4 August 2019.
32. 'Belt and Road Forum for International Cooperation. (2017, April 10). 'Vision and Actions on Jointly Building Belt and Road'. Retrieved from http://beltandroadforum.org/english/n100/2017/0410/c22-45-4.html, accessed on 3 April 2020.
33. Ministry of Education, People's Republic of China.(2009, March 13). 'Circular of the Ministry of Education on Undergraduate Foundation Program for International Students on the Chinese Government Scholarship Program.' Retrieved from http://en.moe.gov.cn/documents/laws_policies/201506/t20150626_191403.html, accessed on 20 November 2020.
34. China Forges Agreement with 54 Countries on Mutual Recognition of Higher Education Degrees. (2020, September 5). *Xinhua Net.* Retrieved from http://www.xinhuanet.com/english/2020-09/05/c_139345581.htm, accessed on 22 November 2020.
35. China Scholar.(n.d.).'China Belt and Road Scholarship.' Retrieved from https://www.china-scholar.com/scholarships/belt-and-road-initiative-scholarships-bri/, accessed on 15 October 2020.
36. Ministry of Culture and Tourism of the People's Republic of China. Retrieved from https://www.mct.gov.cn/, accessed on 17 November 2020.
37. China Tourism Academy (Data Centre for Ministry of Culture and Tourism). Retrieved from http://eng.ctaweb.org.cn/, accessed on 18 November 2020.

Chapter Two

Meaning and Instruments of Soft Power

Introduction

In simple words, International Relations imply the studies of relations amongst nation-states. The nature of these relations is complex to understand. Scholars observe the field of international relations primarily by analysing foreign policies of nation-states. Foreign policy is determined by various factors like geography, economy, leadership, etc. It is evident that a country's foreign policy is directed towards an objective to achieve. Researchers attach the uttermost importance to the concept of power to examine the foreign policy objective.

Power has been the centre of discussion in Political Science in general and in international relations in particular. Politics cannot be detached from power. Scholars acknowledge the inevitability of the concept of power. Such recognition has been evident in the theory and practice of international politics. Baldwin in his '*Power and International Relations*' has argued that, '*Most definitions of politics involve power. Most international interactions are political or have ramifications for politics. Thus, it is not surprising that power has been prominent in discussions of international interaction from Thuycydides to the present day*'.[1] Since its inception in the field of international relations, power has gone through various changes as a concept and as a practice. As a result we have many analysts commenting on it and making it a most debatable concept. Hence it is pertinent here to view various perspectives of power as a concept and practice in international politics. The power-centric analysis of politics has generated interest to study international relations.

Definition of Power

At the outset, we need to be clear on one fact about power that it can be manifested through multiple expressions and cannot be understood by a single dimension. Hence, firstly we will elucidate some definitions of power. According to Robert Dahl '*A has power over B to the extent that he can get B to do something that B would not otherwise do.*'[2] He has pointed out the relational power approach. He has asserted that 'power is a relation.'[3] For Dahl, objects in the relationship of power are actors. These actors could be 'individuals, groups, roles, offices, governments, nation-states, or other human aggregates'.[4]

Bachrach and Baratz have elaborated the concept of power relationship. They opined that power relationship exists when (a) there is a conflict over values or course of action between A and B; (b) B complies with A's wishes; and (c) he does so because he fears that A will deprive him of a value or values which he, B, regards more highly than those which would have been achieved by noncompliance.[5] However, they have paid heed to the dimensions of power like range, domain, and scope to explain the fact that an individual or a nation-state cannot exercise unlimited power.

Morgenthau in his *Politics Among Nations: Struggle for Power and Peace*' maintains that power indicates man's control over the minds and actions of others. He has stated that 'political power is a psychological relationship between those who exercise it and those over whom it is exercised'.[6] He has aptly focused on the psychological aspect of political power and has further argued that we should differentiate between political power and military power. As a strength or as a potential threat, military power adds to the political power of a nation. But when nation-states wage war, they prioritise the military power and thereby renounce the psychological relations which are the crux of political power.

The above-mentioned definitions reflect the relational power approach which takes into consideration the change in the behaviour of a nation-state due to the influence of another nation-state.

Evolution of Power

A study of the evolution of power is an exciting and challenging task. For convenience, one can inspect it in two courses. The first is its evolution as a concept and the second is its evolution through changing resources of exercise.

The Evolution of Power as a Concept

It can be learned with the help of David Baldwin's analysis of power. He has advocated the transformation in the concept of power from an element of national power approach to a relational power approach.

Baldwin has asserted that till the 19th century the field of power analysis was driven by elements of national power approach. It is considered to be the traditional approach. Scholars used these factors to assess the power of a particular country. They contended that the possession of these factors makes a country powerful. Likewise, states having huge militaries were considered to be powerful states. The elements of a national power approach describe power as a possession or property of nation-states. Morgenthau has given a detailed account on elements of national power in his famous book, '*Politics among Nations*'. Hence, as we are considering the elements of national power approach, it is essential to discuss them here. He has identified eight elements of national power such as geography, natural resources, industrial capacity, military capacity, population, national character, national morality, and diplomacy.

Firstly, he has described the significance of geography with examples of America, Great Britain, Italy, and Russia. Then he has commented on the factor of natural resources and discussed the contribution of raw materials in agriculture, industry, and military preparedness. He also mentioned about the significance of oil as a source of energy. Another element is industrial capacity. He has illustrated the example of India whose output of manganese was in millions but the country was lacking in industrial capacity. As manganese is required for steel production, due to inadequate industrial capacity India could not transform its potential power into actual power. According to him, military capacity is also an important element of national power. It can be developed with the qualitative and huge number of armed forces and technological innovations. Morgenthau has noted that new technologies like submarines, tanks, air force, atomic bombs and their appropriate use in war has resulted in success. In addition, he stressed on the quality of military leadership in attaining power.

He has considered population as the element of national power which is vital for the progress of industries, agriculture, and military. He has underscored the role of the population in 18th-century Europe as a source of taxes and employment in the infantry. However, he has suggested that population has to be qualitative in nature. He has also incorporated factors like national character and national morality as the elements of national power. The former refers to a set of values and opinions evolved in a country and the later implies a nation's support to the policies of the government times of peace and war. It includes public opinion on issues like economy, agriculture, and military. Lastly, he has explained the contribution of qualitative diplomacy. Such diplomacy performs the task of integration of the above-mentioned elements. It helps in transforming potential power into actual power. He has pointed out inefficiency of American diplomacy during the inter-war period. In spite of having all the elements of national power, America remained inactive on the international scenario. National character, national morale, and diplomacy are impalpable elements of power.

One has to keep in mind that Morgenthau's scrutiny of power is not only related to elements of a national power approach but also emphasises on relational approach.

Baldwin has observed that addition of various elements of national power is possible which facilitates the measurement of a nation's power.

The majority of realists have understood the power concept in terms of elements of a national power approach. The elements of national power approach 'was challenged during the last half of the twentieth century by the "relational power" approach, developed by scholars working in several disciplines, including psychology, philosophy, sociology, economics, and political science'.[7] The relational power approach deems power as the cause-and-effect relation. For example, A's behaviour at least partially causes a change in B's behaviour. The word 'behaviour' can be interpreted in a wider sense. It covers perspectives, assurances, and choices. The appraisal of a country's power is based on the influence it exerts on another country even if that country's capabilities are declining. In the capability approach, power acts as a strength and in the relational approach it acts as an influence.

The endowment of a relational power approach makes power multi-dimensional in nature which implies the possibility of an increase in one dimension of power with a simultaneous decrease in another. Scholars have illustrated significant dimensions of power. They are as follows:

> Domain refers to the entity over whom power is exercised. Hence, the domain of political power is a group of a people (citizens) obedient to it. We need to be clear with the use of the word 'domain' of power because it has been used to describe different components that make a domain. For example, the domain of the power of the government includes citizens of the country who actively or passively comply with the government's commands. The geographical domain of the power of the government includes even insurgents who are fighting against it. The domain of power of the government could also incorporate resources like land and capital goods. In global politics also, countries have a domain of power which could be varied. Further, it has been observed that countries seek to augment their domain of power. For instance, from the 16th to the 18th centuries, England, France and Germany, in the 20th century the USA and the USSR, and in the 21st century India and China.
>
> The scope of power means several subjects or topics over which power is exercised. In international relations, countries exercise power over multiple issues and a country's power may differ from one issue to another. For example, Japan is economically powerful but lacking in military power.

Weight of power implies a change in the behaviour of one actor due to the influence of another actor. Like a country that has only a 30 per cent chance of achieving its aim in trade negotiations is less powerful than one with a 90 per cent chance.[8] We can derive the weight of power from the country's success in changing the behaviour of another country. Our interpretation of power is based on a relational approach.

Evolution of Power through Changing Resources of its Exercise

Till the 20th century, we find the domination of military resources in global politics. The usage of military resources has vital importance in the realist theories of international relations.

No discourses on power could escape from the theory of realism. After the First World War, a group of scholars were investigating the cause of war to give solutions to prevent it. Those were known as idealist or liberals. After the First World War, they had realised that peace had to be created as it was not a natural condition. Hence, one of the liberals, Woodrow Wilson proposed the establishment of the League of Nations. The League would have military power to stop a potential aggressor from waging war. The Second World War proved the limitations in liberal thinking. It demonstrated the failure of the League of Nations. In this context, realists argued that liberals shunned the role of power, exaggerated the rationality of human beings, wrongly believed that nation-states shared a set of common interests, and were positive about the ability of human beings to overcome the sufferings of war.

Historians of International Relations describe a great debate that occurred in the late 1930s and early 1940s between inter-war liberals and a new generation of realist writers, which included E. H. Carr, Hans. J. Morgenthau, Reinhold Niebuhr, and others, all of whom emphasised the omnipresence of power and the competitive nature of politics among nation-states.

The realist theory of international relations has progressed through various phases like classical realism, structural realism, and neoclassical realism. Thucydides, Machiavelli, and Morgenthau are classical realists.

Waltz and Mearsheimer belong to the group of structural realists and Zakaria adheres to neoclassical realism.

For realists, human nature is competitive, dominant, and fearful. Human beings are power-driven animals. This behaviour gets reflected in the conduct of nation-states. According to Morgenthau, the desire to dominate, in particular, is discernible in all human associations, from family to professional associations and from local political organisations to the state. In realist thought, the state is the fundamental unit of international politics. Realists have identified the difference between domestic politics and international politics. There is a government or an authority to deal with conflicts at the domestic level. T. Dunne, and B.C. Schmidt claim that domestic politics is often described as a hierarchical structure in which different political actors stand in various relations of super- and sub-ordination.[9] But there is anarchy at the international level. Anarchy means that international politics happens in an arena that does not have an all-embracing central authority above the sovereign states. Hence, all nation-states are involved in the struggle for power for survival. Only a powerful state can prevail in this struggle. It is evident from the writings of Thucydides on the Peloponnesian war between Athens and Sparta that in order to retain its preponderance the powerful state, in this case, Athens, had invaded Sparta, the weaker state, which compelled Sparta to retreat for its survival. Realists define power in terms of military strategy. In their view, the international system is shaped by security and survival. Therefore, nation-states prioritise self-defence. As a result, military power occupies a crucial place in world politics. States should take care of their own safety and security. They should not sacrifice their national interests to promote the interests of others. Further, state leaders can adopt immoral ways to maintain their state's security like spying and cheating. Machiavelli has advised the king to follow immoral ways to sustain a power struggle.

In a situation of a struggle for power, the question arises how states manage their survival. There are two options according to realists. First, it is good for states to increase their capabilities in the form of military and economic power. Second is to be the part of the balance of power. It indicates that if a state or a group of weaker states is frightened by a domineering state or a group of stronger states, then the weaker states should join forces and form and alliance and strive to protect their independence by keeping a check on the power of the opposite side. Experts often illustrate the balance-of-power system by giving examples of the Cold War between the USA and the USSR and their military blocs, NATO and WARSAW, respectively.

Though structural realists concede the inevitability of power politics among nation-states, they insist that anarchical condition and relative distribution of power at the international level is the cause of a constant struggle for power.[10] Classical realists advocate human behaviour as the origin of a power conflict. Neo-realists view the nuclear testing of India and Pakistan as a consequence of anarchy or the lack of a central authority to impose rules and maintain order in the system. America-China relations could be explained on a similar basis.

Since the end of the Cold War, a group of scholars have tried to move beyond the meagre assumptions of structural realism and included a number of factors placed at the individual and domestic level into their illustration of international politics. These factors are domestic environment, state leaders, and the relationship between government and citizens. Scholars who have developed such an outlook are known as neo-classical realists. Classical and neo-realists differ in perception of power and particularly military power, but they accept its rudimentary place in international politics.

Currently, there is a decline in the number of inter-state wars but new security threats like terrorism and intra-state conflicts are growing—for instance, Syria, Iraq and Nigeria. Realists opine that force is necessary to deal with such crises.

Experts pay attention to the shift in resources to employ power. Today, non-state actors like transnational corporations that are lacking in military power nevertheless hold paramount economic resources. In realism, states give weightage to military strength for their own security. However, now a days, security concerns are changing. Some observers have argued that the sources of power are, in general, moving away from the emphasis on military force and conquest that marked earlier eras. In assessing international power today, factors such as technology, education, and economic growth are becoming more important, whereas geography, population, and raw materials are becoming less important.[11] Soft power resources have got attention. Military resources help the country in achieving its objective through compulsion. Joseph Nye states that soft power provides legitimacy to a country's policy. As a result, other countries want what that country wants. According to him, when one country gets other countries to want what it wants, it might be called co-optive or soft power in contrast with the hard or command power of ordering others to do what it wants.[12]

Soft Power

The term was systematised by Joseph Nye in the context of the end of the Cold War to estimate American power as with the disintegration of the Soviet wall, America was locating its place in world politics. International politics was going through drastic changes. There was an increase in interdependence. Hence, there was a revision in power distribution. On the top board of classic interstate military issues, the USA is indeed the only superpower with a global military reach, and it makes sense to speak in traditional terms of uni-polarity or hegemony. However, on the middle board of interstate economic issues, the distribution of power is multi-polar. The USA cannot obtain the outcomes it wants on trade, antitrust, or financial regulation issues without the agreement of the European Union, Japan, China, and others. It makes little sense to call this American hegemony. And on the bottom board of transnational issues like terrorism, international crime, climate change, and the spread of infectious diseases, power is widely distributed and chaotically organised among state and non-state actors.[13] Other prominent thinkers who have implicitly articulated soft power are Foucault, Bourdieu, Gramsci, and Habermas.

Several other scholars have also contributed to the soft power narrative from a variety of perspectives and contexts. David Leheny, for instance, traces the conceptual origins of the modern notion of soft power to debate the American decline in the late 1980s and early 1990s, in which the USA's 'soft power' advantage was highlighted for offsetting anxieties about its material decline compared with a more eminent Japan. Steven Lukes argues that power need not be 'blunt' and can influence the formation of preferences in its own way. Gallarotti, on the other hand, posits the theory of 'cosmopolitan power' by employing tenets from three main paradigms of IR-realism (power), neo-liberalism (cooperation) and constructivism (norms)'.[14] As a practice, soft power is an old phenomenon. In order to promote its culture and language France has established the Alliance Francaise in 1883. Similarly, even Germany had formed Goethe Institute in 1951 to spread its culture and language. It is Joseph Nye Jr. who first systematised the term 'soft power' and illustrated it through the series of his books like *Bound to Lead: The Changing Nature of American Power* published in 1990, *The Paradox of American Power: Why the World's Only Superpower Can't Go it Alone* published in 2001 and *Soft Power: Means to Success in World Politics* published in 2012.

According to Joseph Nye, soft power rests on the ability to shape the preferences of others. At the personal level, we are all familiar with the power of attraction and seduction. In a relationship of marriage, power does not necessarily reside with the larger partner, but in the mysterious chemistry of attraction.[15] In business management, managers do not always give commands. They apply the power of attraction to make others want what they want them to want. The ability to set preferences can be generated through resources like a charming personality, culture, political values and institutions, and policies which are perceived as legitimate or supported by moral authority. Politicians use soft power in domestic politics.

Joseph Nye has provided a detailed account of soft power. He has stated that, soft power is not just the same as influence because influence can be created on the basis of hard power like threats or payments. Nor is it just a persuasion as it is much more than the ability to change one's mind by argument. Although persuasion is an important component of it there is something unique about soft power. It is also the ability to entice and attract. In behavioural terms, soft power is an attractive power. In terms of resources, soft power resources are the assets that produce such attraction.[16] Though attraction is the hallmark of soft power, it is not its only attribute. By elaborating on the difference between hard and soft power, one can get another feature of soft power. A country can use threats and economic sanctions to command another country, or it can motivate another country by giving economic help. Here, a country exhibits hard power. Hard power uses tangible resources but in case of soft power, the country's behaviour is shaped by discernible but intangible attraction.

He noted that the common aspect of hard and soft power is that they develop the ability to fulfil one's purpose by changing the behaviour of others. However, he points out that the distinction between them is one of degree, both in the nature of the behaviour and in the tangibility of the resources.[17] Command power can be based on carrots or sticks. Co-optive power can rest on the attraction of one's ideas or on the ability to set the political agenda in a way that shapes the preferences expressed by others.[18] The types of behaviour between command and co-option range along a spectrum from coercion to economic inducement to agenda setting to pure attraction. Soft power resources tend to be associated with the co-optive end of the spectrum of behaviour, whereas hard power resources are usually associated with command behaviour.[19]

In global politics, the resources that engender soft power come from the values of a country which are exhibited in its culture, in the examples it provides by its domestic practices and policies, and in the manner it handles its foreign relations. Joseph Nye has briefly mentioned the advantage of soft power. When countries make their power legitimate in the eyes of others, they encounter less resistance to their wishes. If a country's culture and ideology are attractive, others willingly follow. If a country can shape international rules that are consistent with its interests and values, its actions will more likely appear legitimate in the eyes of others. If it uses institutions and follows rules that encourage other countries to channel or limit their activities in ways it prefers, it will not need as many costly carrots and sticks.[20]

Sources of Soft Power

The soft power of a country rests primarily on three resources: its culture (in places where it is attractive to others), its political values (when it lives up to them at home and abroad), and its foreign policies (when they are seen as legitimate and having moral authority.).[21]

Culture

Nye's discussion on sources of soft power begins with culture. It includes an array of values and practices that brings meaning for a society. It has many expressions. One can distinguish between high culture like literature, art and education, which is fascinating to elites, and popular culture, which emphasises on mass entertainment. When a country's culture is comprehensive and its policies promote values and interests that are shared by others, the possibility of obtaining its desired outcomes would increase because it develops attraction. For example, America has benefited from a universalistic culture. The parochial values and cultures are unlikely to produce soft power.

Some observers regard soft power as solely a popular cultural power. They make the mistake by equating soft power with cultural resources that sometimes help to produce it. For instance, it is said that the North Korean dictator, Kim Jong II used to like pizza and American videos, but that did not influence his nuclear programs. Superb wines and cheeses do not assure attraction for France, nor does the popularity of Pokémon games guarantee that Japan will achieve the policy outcomes it wants. Nonetheless, it does not mean that popular culture is an insignificant resource of soft power. The fact is the efficacy of any power resource depends on the context. For instance, tanks cannot be a great military power resource in marshlands or jungles. If a country lacks an industrial capability, then coal and steel cannot be major power resources.

There are different ways through which culture can be exhibited like personal contacts, visits, and exchanges. The ideas and values that America exports in the minds of more than half a million foreign students who study every year in American universities and then return to their home countries, or in the minds of Asian entrepreneurs who return home after succeeding in Silicon Valley, tend to reach elites with power.[22] It is interesting to know how the former USSR had used culture as a soft power resource. It displayed the supremacy of its cultural and educational systems and spent huge amounts on the arts. It also invested excessively in sports, and over the decades in the Winter Games, Soviet Olympic teams won more gold medals than the USA and stood second in the Summer Games. However, it has been observed that, during the Cold War, American pop culture had received immense popularity. Soviets had a closed system and they had constantly tried to exclude what they called bourgeois cultural influences. Hence, it had relinquished mass culture and never competed with American films, television, and popular music. Soviet culture was attractive in science and technology, classical music, ballet, and athletics, yet due to the absence of popular cultural exports it could exert only a limited impact.

Further Britain has employed culture to enhance its popularity. For example, Shakespeare, rock band–Beatles, characters like Bertie Wooster and Mr. Bean, James Bond films, and books like 'Lord of the Rings' and 'Harry Potter'. Some opine that the 2012 London Olympics have proven to be a potent exercise in soft power for Britain.[23] Higher education institutes like the University of Oxford, and the University of Cambridge have played a crucial role in spreading Britain's soft power. Besides, English has become the language of global communication and trade. It provides Britain a leverage over its competitors in the soft power field. The British Council is highly active in encouraging English language education abroad. France also carries out vigorous efforts in cultural soft power. Its art, food, sports, and films are popular. The Eiffel Tower and the Louvre Museum make it the most visited destination in the world. France is also proud of its Michelin Star restaurants.

Political Values

The values promoted by the government at the domestic level like democracy, at the international level such as cooperating with others and in foreign relations, for example, advocating peace and human rights strongly shape the choices of others. Governments can attract or deter others with their influence by setting their own examples. The USA manifests its values through its actions and words. Political values like democracy and humanity are appealing but it is not sufficient to just proclaim them like during the

Cold War when the USSR conducted a campaign to convince the rest of the world the benefits of the communist system.

Foreign Policy

Another source of soft power. Similarly, foreign policies strongly affect soft power. The Marshall Plan for European Economic Reconstruction after the end of the Second World War produced goodwill for America. Even the Soviet Union became attractive to many due to it resistance to Hitler, its communist values, and planned economy. Foreign policies that appear to be hypocritical, arrogant, indifferent to opinion of others, or based on a narrow approach to national interests can undermine soft power.[24] For instance, the Soviet attack on Hungary in 1956 and Czechoslovakia in 1968 damaged its image as an anti-imperial force. Currently, scholars have pointed out the causes for the decline in American influence.—the Iraq War 2003 and its withdrawal from the Paris Agreement on Climate Change.

Though Europe has experienced long history of wars, it has emerged as a land of peace and prosperity which has created a positive image in many parts of the world. It has been observed that mainly young populations are attracted towards European domestic policies. For example, European policies on climate change, capital punishment, gun control, and the rights of homosexuals are possibly closer to the opinions of many younger people in rich countries. Europe receives trust due to its positions on global climate change, international law, and human rights.

Role of Public Diplomacy

Any discussion on soft power is incomplete without public diplomacy. It plays an important role in channelising the resources of soft power. The government uses public diplomacy to steer soft power resources. Public diplomacy is employed to communicate with and attract the populations of other countries, rather than merely their governments.[25] Public diplomacy tries to attract by drawing attention to these potential resources through broadcasting, subsidising cultural exports, arranging exchanges, and so forth.[26]

The use of public diplomacy in foreign policy can be sparklingly found in the foreign policy of France during the 17th and 18th centuries. France promoted its culture throughout Europe. French not only became the language of diplomacy but was even used in some foreign courts, such as those of Prussia and Russia. During the French Revolution, France sought to go over the heads of foreign governments and appeal directly to their countries' populations by promoting its revolutionary ideology. After its defeat in the Franco-Prussian War, the French government sought to repair the nation's shattered prestige by promoting its language and literature through Alliance Francaise, which was created in 1883.[27] After the First World War, countries had established offices for public diplomacy. Foreign language broadcasting began with the advent of the radio in the 1920s. In the 1930s, the Soviet Union, Germany and Italy competed to promote positive images of their countries and ideologies to foreign populations.

There are three facets of public diplomacy. The first and most immediate dimension is daily communications, which involves explaining the context of domestic and foreign policy decisions. After making decisions, government officials in modern democracies usually devote a good deal of attention to what and how to tell the press. But they generally focus on the domestic press. The foreign press has to be an important target for the first stage of public diplomacy.[28] The second facet is strategic communication, in which a set of simple themes is developed, much like what occurs in a political or advertising campaign.[29] The third dimension of public diplomacy is the development of lasting relationships with key individuals over many years through scholarships, exchanges, training, seminars, conferences, and access to media channels. Over time, about seven hundred thousand people, including two hundred heads of governments, have participated in American cultural and academic exchanges, and these exchanges helped to educate world leaders like Anwar Sadat, Helmut Schmidt, and Margaret Thatcher. Other countries have similar programs.[30]

'It is no coincidence that the discourse on soft power should have emerged in the USA, the world's most powerful country in economic, political, and military terms. Its hard power is expressed in its more than

1,000 military bases across the globe and its enormous defence budget ($ 852 bn in 2012), spending more than the next 17 countries combined. It is American hard power that impacts many countries and helps to spread the American way of life, promoted through its formidable soft power reserves—from Hollywood entertainment giants to the digital empires of the Internet age'[31]. 'In terms of non-state soft power, the USA is also home to the world's highest ranking corporations, best-known think tanks, top non-governmental organisations, and crucially, Ivy League universities, with an innovative and sophisticated research and development record unsurpassed by any other country'.[32]

Nye has exclusively elaborated American foreign policy in the context of soft power. According to him, America had a late entry in the execution of soft power. President Woodrow Wilson established the Committee on Public Information in 1917. In the context of augmenting Germany's propaganda in Latin America, the inter-war period saw American efforts to enhance its soft power ability to prevent Germany's influence. In 1938, the State Department had set up the Division of Cultural Relations to boost American culture in Latin America. During the Second World War, the American government had established two offices: Office of Wartime Information (OWI) and Office of Strategic Services to create a positive image of America. 'Radio played a significant role. What became known as the Voice of America grew rapidly during World War Second. Modelled on the BBC's approach, by 1943 it had 23 transmitters delivering news in 27 languages.[33]

In the post Second World War era, entertainment networks helped in circulating the USA's image as a victor against fascism and a materially prosperous nation. Unlike monotonous Socialist propaganda, America's consumer-based culture did popularise the message of freedom and democracy. Newly independent countries of Asia, Middle East, and Africa had also advocated the notion of freedom. During the Cold War, the Voice of America (VOA), became an important element of US public diplomacy. It was used to support President Truman's 'Campaign for Truth' against Communism and to justify U.S. involvement in the Korean War.[34] Other means of communication included exhibitions, conferences as well as books, films, research scholarships, educational and cultural exchange programmes and so on. Hence, it can be stated that during the Cold War, American soft power strategy was framed to counter the USSR's influence in various parts of the world, for example Hollywood movies, American companies, radio. Wartime soft-power resources emerged from both government and non-government sectors. From the above description, it is evident that America had used public diplomacy effectively throughout the Cold War.

According to Daya Kishan Thussu, due to country-specific approaches and ideologies there can be difference in the nature of soft power and its execution. Nye's analysis of soft power is derived primarily from American experience. Therefore, Thussu has suggested that there is an increasing need to scrutinise universal applicability and to 'de-Americanise' the discussion on soft power.[35]

Soft Power of China

'China's rise is viewed with concern by nation-states influenced by the realist school of thought. According to realists, a rising power is a threat since driven by its expanding national interests the power will pursue a revisionist approach for increasing influence beyond its borders. While not being an exception, China has been remarkably pragmatic in fashioning ambitions. Keen on playing a major role in global affairs without irking international displeasure, it has relied on 'soft' engagement. China's rapid strategic elevation has been accompanied by its emphasis on 'peace and development' and cooperation with neighbours ostensibly for allying fears about an assertive China. The contemporary Chinese foreign policy, both in its global and regional dimensions, is distinct in portraying China as a peace-loving, people-based, cooperative, tolerant, confident and responsible power. Beijing appears convinced that soft power diplomacy will not only enhance its global status but also ensure peace and stability in the neighbourhood for maintaining its rapid economic progress—crucial for cementing itself in the great power league'.[36]

Roots of Soft Power in Chinese Philosophy

The use of soft power in China's foreign policy can be traced to ancient times in Chinese philosophy. Traditional Chinese philosophy mostly originated during the spring and the autumn era (771-476 BC), a period also known as the 'Hundred Schools of Thought', and characterised by several significant cultural and intellectual developments. Till date, the thoughts and ideas of this period hold their influence and soft power is one such idea.[37]

This book tries to examine the hypothesis that China has developed its own notion of soft power. It is using soft power instruments to create convergence of its own national interests with that of others. It can be stated that China traces the roots of its soft power notion in Chinese philosophy. For convenience, this study can be divided into two sections. The first section brings out the core features of Chinese philosophy. The second deals with an interpretation of the instruments of Chinese soft power with reference to the core tenets of Chinese philosophy.

The Core Features of Chinese Philosophy

At the outset, it is necessary to describe an observation of scholars on Chinese philosophy. It can be helpful for us to construct the notion of Chinese soft power. The discussions of ethics in Chinese philosophy almost always engage with issues at the level of practical application; these may differ from stage to stage or vary from person to person according to ability. This does not mean that Chinese philosophers did not consider abstract matters.[38] Less attention was paid to discussions about universal or normative standards and principles. The early Chinese thinkers recognised that while there are norms of action and behaviour, they must invariably be adapted to their contexts of application by particular individuals. For them, the basic problem was not to devise norms or standards for action but how they could be applied by different people in different situations. The primary moral question in Chinese philosophy is not what I ought to do but what is the best way to live?[39]

Humanism: Humanism was an outgrowth, not of speculation, but of historical and social change. The conquest of the Shang (1751-1112 B.C.) by the Chou in 1111 B.C. began a transition from tribal society to a feudal one. To consolidate the empire, the Chou challenged human ingenuity and ability, cultivated new trades and talents, and encouraged the development of experts from all levels of society. Prayers for rain were gradually replaced by irrigation. Ti, formerly the tribal lord, became the god for all. Man and his activities were given greater importance. The time finally arrived when a slave became a prime minister. Humanism, in gradual ascendance, reached its climax in Confucius.[40]

The principle of the Mandate of Heaven was developed by the Chau to validate the rightfulness of their regime. According to this doctrine, man's destiny—both mortal and immortal—depended, not upon the existence of a soul before birth or after death nor upon the whim of a spiritual force, but upon his own good words and good deeds. The Chou asserted, therefore, that the Shang, though they had received the mandate to rule, had forfeited it because they failed in their duties. The mandate then passed on to the founders of the Chou, who deserved it because of their virtue. Obviously, the future of the house of Chou depended upon whether the future rulers were virtuous.[41]

Self-Cultivation: The Chinese word for self-cultivation is Xiushen. According to early Chinese thinkers, the objective of learning was to improve oneself and society. They discuss different notions of self-cultivation. 'For them, the cultivated person was a person who could legitimately lead the people.[42] There is an entire chapter devoted to Xiushen in the Mozi text, associated with Mohism, with reference to Xiushen. Its author indicates it is the development of a devotion to benefit the word.

'*Harmony*:'[43] The conceptual discussion on harmony arose in the backdrop of social instability. Confucius and Mohists had different perspectives on Harmony. Confucius had advocated inter-relations in society to maintain harmony and the Mohists were for bringing standardisation. Daoist thought differs from these two. The Daoist vision of harmony could be analysed as a notion of Chinese soft power. Daoists do not believe in the elimination of individual differences as a precondition for harmony. On the contrary, Daoists consider harmony as a lively exchange between different points of opinions. Daoist philosophy aspires for an ultimate coming together—inclusivity—to be more precise, plurality.

'*Change*:'[44] Chinese philosophy has postulated inter-connectedness between individuals. It argues that change takes place in the context of inter-connectedness. It does not occur in segregation. 'Whether directly or indirectly, individuals may be affected by changes in their environments. This means that individuals are exposed to much that is beyond their immediate control. Likewise, their impact and influence on others can extend beyond what is immediately obvious or directly quantifiable. This is the theory of ganying, mutual resonance. The notion of mutual resonance crystalises the concept of interdependent selfhood, capturing the susceptibility of individuals to factors external to their being and beyond their immediate control, as well as their power to affect others'.[45]

Confucian Philosophy

The '*Analects*'[46] of Confucius is considered as a key text for Confucius's ideas. The text consists of pieces not written by Confucius himself but arranged by his first and second-generation disciples and accumulated over a period of time roughly seventy years after his death. At the outset, it is essential to mention that 'Confucius did not think that there could be a universal definition for any moral concept, which would be applicable to everyone in every situation. When students asked him to explain an ethical principle, Confucius would give an answer appropriate to each one's particular strengths, shortcomings, or personal background'.[47] Such an approach would rather bring flexibility in analysing of roots of the Chinese notion of soft power in Confucian philosophy.

Through his '*Analects*', Confucius has strived to generate the idea of the ideal man by explaining maxims like humanity and superior man. The following is a description of a few *Analects*. It would assist one in theorising the Chinese notion of soft power.

If a ruler places himself right, he will be obeyed without his command. If he fails to place himself right, his commands will not be followed.

A man who reviews the old so as to find out the new is qualified to teach others.[48]

Only the man of humanity knows how to love people and hate people.[49]

The superior man prefers to be slow in word but rigorous in action.

R. Eno, in his book, *The Analects of Confucius—The Online Teaching Translation states that* do not be concerned that no one recognises your merits. Be concerned that you may not recognise those of others.[50]

According to W. T. Chan, when a substance exceeds refinement, one becomes rude. When refinement exceeds substance, one becomes urbane. It is only when one's substance and refinement are properly blended that he becomes a superior man. He further states that the superior man brings the good facets of others to completion and does not encourage the bad facets of others. The superior man is broadminded but not partisan; the inferior man is partisan but not broadminded.[51]

Do not impose upon others what you yourself do not desire is known as the golden rule of Confucius.[52] It is contradictory to the golden rule of Christianity which says, '*Do unto others as you would have them do unto you*'.[53] The Christian rule guides one what to do and the Chinese rule states what one should not do.

Chinese philosophers pay less attention to universal principles. They state that behavioural norms and actions must be adapted according to the context by the concerned individual. This line of thought could be observed in China's foreign policy. China renders economic assistance to countries irrespective of the nature of their political systems. Contrarily, America's assistance comes with terms and conditions in the form of application of universal principles like democracy and human rights. The same example could be applicable for the principle of Harmony which implies lively interchange between different points of views. China builds and maintains bilateral relationship with countries of different kinds of political systems.

With respect to the principle of the Mandate of Heaven, it could be argued that China's soft power strategy towards South Asia, Southeast Asia, Africa, and Latin America revolves around the principle of good words and good deeds. Beijing's involvement in South Asian countries consists of different elements such as economic engagement, infrastructure, humanitarian assistance, people-to-people communication, education, and state visits. Hence, 'economic initiatives combined with enhanced people-to-people communication are aimed at creating a 'Virtuous' China'.[54]

China has signed FTAs with ASEAN and Pakistan. China's FTAs with Bangladesh, Nepal and Sri Lanka are under process. South Asia's deficient infrastructure, particularly poor physical connectivity, has been a major hindrance to the growth of intra-regional trade and commerce. Lack of good roads, ports, advanced telecommunications networks and adequate electricity is conspicuous across the region. The infrastructure deficit has allowed China the opportunity of creating strategic space and goodwill in the region by assisting individual countries in creating new infrastructure capacities[55] like the China-Pakistan Economic Corridor, Matara-Beliatta section of the Matara-Kataragama Railway Extension Project, Lotus communication tower in Sri Lanka, and the Bangladesh-China-Myanmar Economic Corridor.

In Southeast Asia, China has been active in building a benign-constructive image in the region given its importance as a neighbour.[56] China has helped Southeast Asian countries during the Asian financial crisis by refraining from devaluing its currency. China has also concluded an FTA with ASEAN. China's White Papers on Peaceful Development ensure the peaceful nature of China's growth.[57]

The concept of self-cultivation is evident in the Belt and Road initiative. According to Chinese philosophy, only a self-cultivated man can lead the world. China's eastern provinces benefited from economic reforms. However, it created regional disparity between the western and eastern provinces. The Chinese government has initiated the Western Development

Strategy to improve the economic conditions of the western regions by building infrastructure projects. The BRI aims at establishing the infrastructure in different continents and it would also help grow the Chinese economy. The vision and action of the BRI has highlighted its advantages for Xinjiang province. It will act as a window of westward opening-up to deepen communications and cooperation with Central, South and West Asian countries.[58] Hence, one can argue that the BRI is a Chinese attempt of self-cultivation to lead the world.

Thoughts of Confucius are also being reflected in Chinese foreign policy. 'The superior man wants to be slow in word but diligent in action' is discernible in the pro-activeness in China's foreign policy for example, in its bilateral relations and its participation in multilateral forums. Through policies like the BRI, China is fulfilling its national interests and trying to create the convergence of its interests with that of others. So, it does not involve forceful strategies. Such behaviour complies with the Golden Rule of Confucius: 'Do not impose upon others what you yourself do not desire'.

Conclusion

The concept of soft power is associated with Joseph Nye. He has defined it as a country's ability to attract others. He has also provided the sources of soft power like culture, values, and foreign policy. He has explained the term in the context of the disintegration of the USSR. He has suggested that America should consider the changing nature of power equations at the international level and argued that in a multi-polar world, a country cannot just rely on hard power however it must use culture, values, and foreign policy to achieve the national interest.

China is relatively a newcomer in the field of soft power. Since 1978, China has been active in foreign policy. After the Tiananmen Square crackdown in 1989, 'the Chinese leadership began consciously integrating with the international community with its scholars participating more actively in the global discourse on international relations, including soft power'.[59] 'The expansion of the dynamic domain of soft power for increasing national appeal through a careful combination of culture and economics, both as a distinct alternative to mainstream Western notions prevailing in modern times'.[60] Therefore, it can be stated that China traces its notion of soft power back to Chinese philosophy and uses trade, investment and culture and language as instruments of Chinese soft power.

NOTES

1. Baldwin, D. A. (2013). 'Power and International Relations.' In W. Carlsnaes, T. Risse, & Beth. A. Simmons (eds.), *Handbook of International Relations.* London: Sage Publications Ltd., p. 273.
2. Dahl, R. A. (1957). The Concept of Power. *Behavioural Science*, 2 (3), 201-215. Retrieved from https://welcometorel.files.wordpress.com/2008/08/conceptpower_r-dahl.pdf, accessed on May 16, 2017.
3. Ibid.
4. Ibid.
5. Bachrach, P. & Baratz, M. S. (1963). 'Decisions and Non decisions: An Analytical Framework.' *The American Political Science Review,* 57(3), pp. 632-642. Retrieved from https://www.jstor.org/stable/1952568, accessed on February 13, 2017.
6. Morgenthau, H. J. (1948). *Politics among Nations: The Struggle for Power and Peace.* New York: Alfred A. Knopf, p. 14.
7. Baldwin, op. cit., p. 274.
8. Ibid.
9. Dunne, T. & Schmidt, B. C. (2008). 'Realism.' In J. Baylis, S. Smith & P. Owens. (eds). *The Globalization of World Politics: An Introduction to International Relations.* New York: Oxford University Press, p. 93.
10. Ibid.
11. Nye Jr, J. S. (1990). 'The Changing Nature of World Power.' *Political Science Quarterly,* 105(2), pp. 177-192. Retrieved from https://www.jstor.org/stable/2151022, accessed on 20 February 2017.
12. Nye Jr, J. S (1990). 'Soft Power.' *Foreign Policy,* 80, pp. 153-171. Retrieved from https://www.jstor.org/stable/1148580, accessed on 17 January 2017.
13. Nye Jr, J. S. (2012). *Soft Power: The Means to Success in World Politics.* New Delh: KW Publishers Pvt. Ltd. p. 4.
14. Palit, P. S. (2017). *Analysing China's Soft Power Strategy and Comparative Indian Initiative.* New Delhi: Sage Publications India Pvt. Ltd. p. 4.
15. Nye Jr, J. S. (2012), op. cit., p. 5.
16. Nye Jr, J. S. (2008). 'Public Diplomacy and Soft Power.' *Annals of the American Academy of Political and Social Science,* 616, pp. 94-109. Retrieved from https://www.jstor.org/stable/25097996, accessed on 20 February 2017.
17. Nye Jr, J. S. (2012), op. cit., p. 7.
18. Nye Jr, J. S. (1990), 'The Changing Nature of World Power,' op. cit., p. 181.
19. Nye Jr, J. S. (2012), op. cit., p. 7.
20. Ibid.

21. Nye Jr, J. S. (2008), op. cit., p. 96.
22. Nye Jr, J. S. (2012), op. cit., p. 13.
23. Urban, M. (2012, August 13). 'Will Olympics Prove a Bargain for UK Soft Power Gains? *BBC News*. Retrieved from https://www.bbc.com/news/uk-19250118, accessed on 15 March 2021.
24. Nye Jr, J. S. (2012), op. cit., p. 14.
25 Nye Jr, J. S. (2008), op. cit., p. 95.
26. Ibid.
27. Nye Jr, J. S. (2012), op. cit., p. 100.
28. Nye Jr, J. S. (2008), op. cit., p. 101.
29. Nye Jr, J. S. (2012), op. cit., p. 108.
30. Nye Jr, J. S. (2008), op. cit., p.102.
31. Thussu, D. K. (2016). *Communicating India's Soft Power: Buddha to Bollywood.* Sage/ Vistaar. p. 17.
32. Ibid.
33. Nye Jr, J. S. (2012), op. cit., p. 102.
34. Bernhard, N. (n.d.). 'President Harry Truman Enlisted Journalists in Cold War: Are there Parallels Between then and now?' Nieman Reports. Retrieved from https://niemanreports.org/articles/president-harry-truman-enlisted-journalists-in-the-cold-war/, accessed on 2 June 2021.
35. Thussu, op. cit., p. 17.
36. Palit, op. cit., pp. 25-26.
37. Ibid.
38. Lai, K. L. (2008). *An Introduction to Chinese Philosophy*. New York: Cambridge University Press. p. 5.
39. Ibid.
40. Chan, W. T. (1963). *A Source Book in Chinese Philosophy*. New Jersey: Princeton University Press. p. 3.
41. Ibid.
42. Lai, op. cit., pp. 4-5.
43. Ibid.
44. Ibid.
45. Ibid.
46. Chan, op. cit., p. 14.
47. Liu, J. L. (2006). *An Introduction to Chinese Philosophy: From Ancient Philosophy to Chinese Buddhism.* UK: Blackwell Publishing. p. 48.
48. Chan, op. cit., p. 23.
49. Ibid.
50. Eno, R. (2015). 'The Analects of Confucius—The Online Teaching Translation. p. 4. Retrieved from https://chinatxt.sitehost.iu.edu/Analects_of_Confucius_(Eno-2015).pdf, accessed on 20 August 2021.
51. Chan, op. cit., p. 29.

52. Liu, op. cit., p. 53.
53. Ibid.
54. Palit, op. cit., p. 47.
55. Ibid.
56. Ibid.
57. The State Council, The People's Republic of China. (2011, September 6). *China's Peaceful Development.* Retrieved from http://english.www.gov.cn/archive/white_paper/2014/09/09/content_281474986284646.htm, accessed on 15 June 2017.
58. Belt and Road Forum for International Cooperation. (2017, April 10). *Vision and Actions on Jointly Building Belt and Road* Retrieved from http://beltandroadforum.org/english/n100/2017/0410/c22-45-4.html, accessed on 3 April 2020.
59. Palit, op. cit., p. 29.
60. Ibid.

Chapter Three

Trade as an Instrument of Soft Power

Introduction

The Chinese Communist Party's legitimacy is based on domestic economic growth. Since the establishment of the PRC, Chinese leaders have emphasised economic progress. Mao Zedong had advocated 'Politics in Command'; however, his policy of the Great Leap Forward is centred on economic development. In 1978, China had opened its economy to the rest of the world under the paramount leadership of Deng Xiaoping. Later, successive leaders have also paid attention to the betterment of the economy.

In the mid-1990s China displayed its military strength by sending ships to the disputed South China Sea. It also appealed to countries in Southeast Asia to renounce their cooperation with America. This strategy had produced unfavourable effects for China. Southeast Asian countries had criticised Beijing and consolidated their military relations with America. It brought American armed forces close to Beijing. In 1998, during the Asian financial crisis, it helped Southeast Asian countries which formed a positive image of China. Ultimately Beijing had realised that its military power was relatively weak and the economic card would generate more benefits than military action. Besides, the process of China's continuous economic rise coincided with increasing interdependence at the global level. Therefore, on the one hand, there was an optimistic environment for trade due to economic progress and on the other, recognition of economic cooperation compelled Beijing to focus on trade as an essential component of China's foreign policy.

The Evolution of Chinese Economy since 1978

Many scholars would agree on the fact that once upon a time China was at the apex in the field of world economy and technological development. It was known as the 'Middle Kingdom,' the centre around which all else revolved.[1] However, from the 18th century onwards, China became vulnerable abroad and disintegrated at home. The Chinese people witnessed acute poverty. For instance, as late as the early 1980s, more than 100 million Chinese had to subsist on an annual income that was less than the cost of a good dinner in New York.[2] The phenomena of '*one pants family*" was prevalent in Chinese society. It implied that a family possessed only one set of clothes for one member.[3]

Under the leadership of Deng Xiaoping, economic reforms were introduced in 1979 which led to the elimination of poverty. From the 1990s, it became the fastest-growing economy. According to Overholt, considering factors like huge territory and overpopulation, China's economic advancement is remarkable. Unlike China, other countries which have exhibited rapid economic progress are Hong Kong, Singapore (small countries) South Korea and Japan (homogeneous countries) and Saudi Arabia (under-populated country). Therefore, it would be an exciting work to describe the progress of the Chinese economy since the 1980s.

In the late 19th century, the great powers had imposed an Open Door Policy on China to acquire equal access to the Chinese market. After 1949, the USA had imposed an embargo on China. Besides, in the early 1950s, China had accepted the Soviet 'two bloc' view that there were two separate markets, capitalist and socialist, and that the latter was stronger.[4] In the 1960s, the USSR had tried to inflict the international division of labour in socialist markets. China had rejected it by describing it as a form of covert imperialism. Mao vehemently backed the principle of self-reliance.

By the end of the Seventies, China's relatively modest growth rate constituted something of an exception in East Asian countries like Japan,

South Korea, Taiwan, Singapore, and Hong Kong who were experiencing economic progress. China faced unique problems, in particular, its vastness and diversity, together with the legacy of civil war, turmoil and occupation. In addition, it had been isolated, a condition partly self-imposed and partly the result of an American embargo, plus the withdrawal of all Soviet aid and personnel in 1959.[5]

The post-Mao leadership initiated the 'New Open Door Policy' in the late 1970s in response to the two-decades-old closed economic system. Gittings is of the opinion that China's economic reforms indicate its aspiration to participate in the international market. Since the early 1980s, China had welcomed the 'One World' vision of international trade.

Economic reforms in China have engendered different opinions. Scholars have linked China's Open Door policy of 1978 to Chinese nationalism. They have argued that the Open Door policy became an instrument of nationalism. The Chinese people began to describe economic reforms as 'Socialism with Chinese characteristics'.[6] Through the 1984 agreement with Britain on Hong Kong, the Open Door policy also sought to restore the integrity of the Chinese nation, regaining the first territory to be lost to Western semi-colonialism.[7]

Economic reform has drastically transformed the economic, political and social life of China. Reform has given the coastal areas the initiative over the interior (including Beijing) and has put economics above politics in a country whose central post-revolutionary slogan was 'Politics in Command.' It has loosened central control over provinces, the state enterprises, the locus and sectoral thrust of economic activity, and above all, over the individual.[8] A cosmopolitan culture was developed in coastal areas, cities and in universities. Effectively, Marxism was dead.

It is observed that the reform process has been spurred by a combination of the efforts of the central government and the natural desire of the Chinese people and lower-level government units to improve economic institutions for their own benefit.[9] The central government has adopted a gradual and experimental approach. It is useful to keep this general picture in mind when we study China's reform process.

The process of reform began in 1978 with the creation of special economic zones along the south-eastern seaboard, including Guangdong province, in which the rural communes were dismantled and peasants were given control of land on long-term leases and encouraged to market their produce. It was based on a step-by-step piecemeal and experimental approach.[10] It was decided that if a reform worked, it would be executed in new areas; if it failed then it would be renounced.

Deng Xiaoping had visited Guangdong on 11 November 1977. He was briefed on the problem of young men trying to escape across the border from China to Hong Kong. Tens of thousands of youths were risking their lives each year by attempting to run or swim across the border. Until that point, Beijing had regarded the problem as a security issue.[11] As a result, policemen were assigned for patrolling to deal with such incidents. Deng had realised that it would be incorrect to treat such incidents as a security issue. This predicament had emerged due to the disproportionate standards of comfort on both the sides and hence the demand for change among the Chinese.

During Deng's meetings in Guangdong, local officials also complained about the shortage of foreign currency, which was needed to pay for foreign technology and to underwrite construction projects. Deng supported the view that to earn foreign currency they should establish two agriculture collection centres, wherein fruits and vegetables would be collected for export.[12] Further, he suggested promoting hostels and tourist amenities in Guangdong to earn foreign currency. Nowhere did he mention foreign investment.

Consequently, Guangdong became a guinea pig for China's economic transformation. During the reform process, it has turned into the centre of industries which would mass-produce goods for the global market.

Ezra Vogel has unfolded the story of the making of foreign investment in China. Xi Zhongxun (the father of the current Chinese President Xi Jinping) was appointed as a provincial party secretary of Guangdong. He was a key person in the process of opening up Guangdong for foreign investment. On 6 January 1979, Xi had received a green signal from Beijing to draft a letter asking for Beijing's permission to admit foreign investment in Guangdong. He quickly began to frame the proposal. Meanwhile, there was an increase in the demand for scrap metal in Hong Kong for its thriving construction projects. Yuan Geng, the head of the Hong Kong Merchant Steamship Group, had recommended the dismantling of old, unused Chinese ships and vending the scrap to Hong Kong builders. He was in search of a site for such a project. He had offered to put foreign investment in Shekou, an area in Guangdong, as Hong Kong was congested. The establishment of foreign ownership in Shekou is considered a headway for China.

Besides Shekou, SEZs were planned in three other areas in Guangdong—Shenzhen, Zhuhai and Shantou. SEZs were given significant tax breaks and other preferential treatment that would create incentives for foreign investors and stimulate the growth of the export sector.[13] The link between Guangdong and Hong Kong has caused the flow of technology, investment, and management expertise and unmasked the outside world to China.

China had initiated agricultural reforms parallel with industrial reforms. It has been observed that though collectivised agriculture had facilitated irrigation, it has brought heavy starvation. It was awful that in 1978 China did not have enough food for its population. After the 'Great Leap' collectives were reduced and the supply of chemical fertilisers increased to raise production. However, an acute scarcity of food persisted.

In agricultural reform, the government first increased prices for agricultural goods. Second, the previous 'collective farming system' was shifted to the 'household-responsibility system.' Under the new system, each farm household was assigned a fixed quota of grain that the household had to sell to the government at official prices. However, any extra grain the household produced could be sold at market prices. The reforms were implemented gradually and completed in 1984.[14]

There is an interesting story about the agricultural reforms in China. Decentralisation of agriculture was initiated by farmers there. In Anhui province, they had signed a secret document in blood. It stated that they would farm the land as individual families not as communes. They had decided to hide their plan from the higher authorities. Wan Li, a party secretary of Anhui, came to know about it. He told Deng that the peasants were dismantling the people's communes on their own. Deng reportedly told Wan to let the policy unfold. In 1979, Anhui experienced a successful midyear harvest.

Directive No. 75 was issued which allowed the spread of the Anhui model to other suitable areas. In 1958, communes were established to channelise peasants for public works and collective farming. In 1982, they were dismantled. Reforms in agriculture have brought several positive effects. Household production had ended the scarcity of grains and raised the income of peasants. It also led to the growth of industrial crops such as cotton, flax, and tobacco. In 1981, China was the fourth-largest importer of cotton; in 1985, it became an exporter of the same. Rural families, who were encouraged to work hard, could achieve their agreed-grain-production targets and allow their young adults to work in rural industry. Farmers who sold the products in towns and cities, too, improved the quality and quantity of food for urban consumers. Reforms had not only empowered rural peasants but also led to the setting up of light industry.

Xiaodong Zhu has explained the ramifications of increase in agricultural output on employment in China. He has noted that a large number of labourers moved from agriculture to industry due to the increment in food availability. For instance, from 1978 to 1984, the share of agriculture in total employment dropped from 69 to 50 per cent. In simple words, 19 per cent of China's labour force shifted to the non-agricultural sector. It has been observed that these workers preferred to work in rural industrial enterprises also known as Township and Village Enterprises (TVE's). TVE's had contributed to the growth of incomes of rural China between 1980 and 1990.

At present, collectively-owned TVE's have largely disappeared from China's economy and have been replaced by private enterprises located in the more flourishing areas of the country. Both agricultural productivity and structural transformation stagnated in the second half of the 1980s. Starting around 1990, markets for agricultural inputs and outputs were gradually liberalised and government interventions were significantly reduced.[15]

Farming activities which were prohibited during Mao's era were restored. For example, farmers began to raise pigs, chickens, and ducks as well as carry out handicraft production. Any discussion on reforms in agriculture would be incomplete without the topic of ownership of land. Strictly speaking, ownership of land was and still is collective; it belongs to the commune or the village. The right of use belongs to the farmer who is assigned the land. Eventually, the right to use assigned land was guaranteed on a permanent basis and became transferable—hence, the difference between this right to use and ownership is moot. Reform therefore succeeded in allowing private farming to return to the agricultural sector.[16] Hence, the private economy was re-established in the farming sector.

Changes under Deng Xiaoping

One needs to consider the role of Deng Xiaoping in China's economic reforms. To link Mao's legacy with the reforms programmes, Deng aptly used the principle propounded by Mao, 'Seeking Truth from Facts'.[17] It implies the acceptance of result-driven principles and abandonment of non-result driven principles. It makes every idea zestful and evolutionary and brings a realistic approach to public policy. So, seeking truth from facts could be illustrated with the Guangdong and Anhui experiments. Also, it is said that Deng had preferred this doctrine to attain a sharp break from the Cultural Revolution.

Ezra Vogel has mentioned Deng's distinct way of convincing people. He used to apply popular maxims to explain policies. Thereby, he could avoid disagreements and create a benign image of himself. He had explained a 'Cat Theory' to reduce the impact of Mao's ideology. He had stated that the colour of the cat is not important if it grabs the mouse. It indicates that work is more important than ideology. It he had straightway opposed the ideology; it could have invited displeasure. The Chinese were impressed by this 'Cat Theory'.

It can be observed that economic reforms had percolated to different levels of society and Deng had received tremendous support from the Chinese. Workers and managers were contented because of the upliftment of small-scale entrepreneurs and encouragement to light and medium industry. Students and intellectuals were glad on account of freedom in travelling and exchange of thoughts. Though there were cuts in military budgets to back economic reforms, the majority of the military leadership supported him. Communist Party leaders were also promoting reforms.

Moreover, Deng's reforms had some political implications. 'The Universalist, ideological model of the Maoist era was being replaced by something closer to the development model of the East Asian Tigers.'[18] Decentralisation of the state was introduced to facilitate economic progress.

It can be mentioned that the early reforms were an attempt to exploit the human and material resources in China in toto. The economy was in the take-off mode. During the course of time, it emerged as the fastest-growing economy of the world.

Diverse sectors in China have experienced useful as well as gloomy outcomes of reforms. William Joseph in his book, *Politics in China: An introduction* has enunciated that the performance of SOEs in China is relatively poor compared to private firms. The number of SEOs declined drastically immediately after the reforms. As a consequence, 45 million workers became jobless. TVEs were also facing a crisis due to which 20 million TVE employees became unemployed. So, overall, 65 million people were adversely affected. The public sector remained burdened by over-employment, as well as by welfare responsibilities for millions of retirees; the entire sector's profits were close to zero, serving as an enormous drag on the entire economy and government coffers.[19] Hence, in 1997, some small and medium enterprises were privatised.

Nevertheless, SOEs exert influence on the Chinese economy. More than 50 million workers are employed in state-owned and state-controlled enterprises. The state dominates crucial industries such as telecommunications, steel and iron, energy and power, aviation and shipping and defence and they are managed through the State Asset Supervision and Administration Commission.

Privatisation is occupying a vital place in the Chinese economy, mainly after China's entry into the World Trade Organisation. To facilitate the process of privatisation, the PRC had amended its constitution in 1993 and introduced the term 'Socialist Market Economy'. Strikingly, the private sector acquired legitimacy. Hence, experts describe the Chinese system as state capitalism as the state remains the driver of Chinese economy. The emergence of the private sector has challenged the existence of SOEs. During the initial days of reforms, SOEs had 78 per cent of industrial output but in the 1990s their output reduced.

The private sector is confronting obstacles. The number of private entrepreneurs belonging to the Communist Party of China is growing. They are called 'Red Capitalists'. It clearly displays the party's linkage to the private sector. It is based on personal connections and favouritism rather than individual enterprise and initiative. Moreover, the private sector in China does not have access to official sources of credit. It chooses informal financial mechanisms like rotating credit associations, borrowing from family and friends, and creating 'backdoor' relationships with state banks, the SOE's and even disguised private banks.[20]

Consistent with the reforms, restrictions on labour movement was removed. Earlier, the labour policy was driven by plan economy in which the household registration system was practiced. It was also known as the *hukou* system. It implied the restriction of both the movement of the population and the economic mobility of agricultural labour, the exclusion of the rural population from urban welfare systems, and the restriction of rural workers from non-agricultural jobs.[21] Reforms at rural and urban level have helped in labour mobility. The third plenum of the 18th CCP central committee loosened the *hukou* system by permitting open migration to small and medium sized cities.

The fruits of liberalisation of trade and investment in China are notable. A transformation in China's exporting products is evident. In 1986, exports of textiles and clothing were more than the export of crude oil which underlined the change from resource-intensive products to labour-intensive products. In 1995, exports of machinery and electronics had surpassed the export of textiles and clothing. It indicated the transition of traditional labour-intensive exports to non-traditional labour-intensive products. In 2001, China's access to the WTO has increased the exports of high technology.

The success story of liberalisation of trade and investment in China could be examined with the example of China-East Asia economic relations. Sharing an outward looking development strategy with neighbouring economies in East Asia contributed greatly to China's economic success. By becoming engaged with the world economy, China's economy became more efficient and market oriented.[22] Due to a FDI-trade nexus, FDI has been accelerating China's exports, which in turn attracts another inflow of FDIs.

In its early attempts to attract foreign investment, China enticed the Chinese Diaspora concentrated in Hong Kong, Macau, Taiwan and Southeast Asia. Due to China's cheap labour, low-cost land, low taxes, and large domestic market the Chinese Diaspora was anxious to invest in China. In addition, they wished to set up projects in their hometowns to raise the social status of their families. Hence, enterprises coming to China in the 1980s were mainly from ethnic Chinese.

Further, China's economic growth has influenced regional trade. China began to export final demand goods to America, non-durable consumer goods to Japan, and intermediate goods to East Asian countries. Trade was becoming China-centric. For example, manufacturers in America, Japan, Hong Kong, Taiwan and Korea moved their plants to China. Japan and other East Asian countries had increased their exports of intermediate goods to China. Finished products from China and intermediate goods were finally exported to the U.S. market. China's export of clothes and electronics appliance helps imports from Korea, Taiwan, etc.

To boost the inflow of FDI, China created favourable terms for investors. Simultaneously, China was taking enormous diplomatic efforts to normalise relations with Indonesia, Singapore, and Korea. Hence, new investments arrived in China from these countries despite a reduction in FDI inflows from advanced countries after the Tiananmen Square incident in 1989. Besides, China launched its 'Go Out Strategy' to facilitate overseas FDI, particularly in Africa. Finally, China's entry into WTO has become a breakthrough in China's economic progress.

With such a brief introduction of Chinese economy, it is vital to discuss a few facts which highlight its current state. The country's economy expanded at an average rate of 9.5 per cent over last 40 years. Its GDP rose from 367.9 bn Yuan in 1978 to 82.71 trillion Yuan in 2017. The number of rural poor decreased from 770 million to 30.46 million over the past 40 years. The share of its primary, secondary and tertiary sector in 2017 was 7.9, 40.5 and 51.6, respectively. In 1978, foreign trade was $ 20.6 bn; in 2017 it became $ 4.1 trillion. In 1983, FDI was $ 920 million; in 2017 it grew to $ 131 bn. Approximately 30 per cent of the world's economic growth has been credited to China since 2015.

Overall, it can be stated that in China, economic reforms were introduced in different phases and the process is yet to be completed. Reforms were led by leaders such as Deng Xiaoping, Jiang Zemin, Hu Jintao and Xi Jinping. It seems its reforms and foreign policy are interlinked. For instance, the 'Go Out Strategy' which has served its internal economic interests as well as maintained its bilateral relations with other countries.

Notwithstanding all this, there are hurdles in the Chinese economy. First, there is an increasing gap between the rich and the poor, cities and countryside. Second, the Chinese tend to save money. Confucius culture believes in savings. During the Mao era, the Chinese suffered from major economic uncertainty. Currently, there is a lack of health insurance and social security. So, they save some money for emergencies which minimises their consumption capacity. Hence, domestic consumption should be encouraged. Environmental degradation has paved the way for mass uprising.

Undoubtedly, it can be stated that China's domestic economic growth has facilitated its external economic relations. As a result, trade has become a key area of foreign policy. China's bilateral trade has promoted mutual benefits which is conducive to a peaceful environment. In this context, it is engrossing to argue that China is utilising trade as an instrument of soft power. To support the argument, one could illustrate China's Free Trade Agreement (FTA) with different countries.

Rajeev Ahmed in an article titled '*Free Trade Agreement with China: A Necessity*' has aptly pointed out that China's FTA strategy is based on several important considerations such as regional security interests, access to natural resources for uninterrupted development, need to be reckoned as a market economy and to improve access to regional trade networks.[23]

Up to now, China has signed 16 FTAs. Its FTA partners are ASEAN, Singapore, Pakistan, New Zealand, Chile, Peru, Costa Rica, Iceland, Switzerland, the Maldives, Mauritius, Georgia, Korea, Australia, Hong Kong, and Macao.[24]

A few significant FTA engagements are examined below.

China-ASEAN FTA

At the outset, one can elucidate China ASEAN FTA because China has registered the geo-strategic and geo-economic importance of ASEAN, especially after the introduction of the reforms policy. As a consequence, ASEAN, as an entity of Southeast Asian countries, has occupied a central place in China's 'good neighbourhood' policy and 'go global' strategy. The nations making up ASEAN have abundant natural resources provided by tropical geography, ocean and forests. They are the world's largest producers of rubber, palm oil, tin, and *semul* (silk cotton) and important suppliers of rice, petroleum, timber, manganese, and aluminium. Compared to ASEAN, other regions in larger Asia such as Northeast Asia, Central Asia and South Asia are unable to exert influence due to the presence of major powers in their respective regions such as American military presence in North East Asia, Russia in Central Asia and India in South Asia.

China-ASEAN FTA (CAFTA) is not the outcome of a sudden decision. The concept of an 'East Asia Free Trade Area' was floated early at the 1994 ASEAN summit. The ASEAN members had realised that Southeast Asia was only a sub-regional organisation, and it would have to expand its economic sphere to include China, Japan and Korea in order to ensure regional sustainable development.[25] Though at that time it could not become a reality, the ideation of a regional trade zone prevailed. Two factors were responsible for China-ASEAN FTA. Firstly, globalisation which made the regional economic cooperation unavoidable and secondly, ASEAN countries were worried about the competition from China in trade and investment on account of China's WTO entry.

Further China joined the Treaty of Amity and cooperation in Southeast Asia. It acted as a mechanism to build confidence amongst ASEAN countries towards China. 'ASEAN's 1976 Treaty of Amity and co-operation is the grouping's founding non-aggression pact aimed at promoting regional stability'.[26] It does not stop the participants from developing their multidimensional relations and co-operation with other countries.

CAFTA has resulted in the gradual reduction of tariffs on several imported and exported goods. Like Thailand and Malaysia's previous tariff rate upon textile and apparel imports from China averaged 21.5 per cent and 16.8 per cent, and rate dropped to 16.9 per cent and 15 per cent from July 1, 2005, and will drop to 10.6 per cent and 9.2 per cent from January 1, 2007; Vietnam's previous textile tariff rate was 36.6 per cent and it was reduced to 31 per cent after July 2005.[27] In 2007, the Vice President of the World Bank acknowledged the rapid regional trade integration which involves China. Bilateral trade between China and ASEAN countries increased from less than 8 bn US dollars in 1991 to 160.8 bn dollars in 2006.[28]

The China-ASEAN Expo has become a medium in facilitating FTA. In 2008, Gao Hucheng, the then vice-co-chair of the China-ASEAN Expo organising committee and Chinese vice-minister took note of the China-ASEAN Expo. He said that the four rounds of Expo have effectively transformed FTA construction from the paperwork consensus reached by state leaders to pragmatic moves of business circles, which has injected a powerful drive for the FTA's construction. He noted that more than 98 per cent of products which are exhibited in Expo are enumerated in the FTA tariff-reduction program.[29]

Against the backdrop of the international financial crisis of 2008 on 15 August 2009, the Chinese Minister of Commerce and Economic

Ministers of 10 ASEAN member-states signed the ASEAN-China FTA investment agreement.[30] It is considered a remarkable step. It showed their desire for collaboration in dealing with the financial crisis and to pursue trade and investment liberalisation. Though the China-ASEAN FTA is a novel experiment of cooperation for both sides, they were keen in engaging with each other. The timeline of the China-ASEAN FTA proceedings is self-explanatory.

Year	*China-ASEAN FTA Proceedings*
2002	Talks on China-ASEAN Free Trade Area
2003	Execution of Early Harvest Plan
2004	Agreement on Trade in Goods.
2007	Agreement on Trade in Services
2009	ASEAN-China FTA investment agreement

Source: Ministry of Commerce People's Republic of China. http://fta.mofcom.gov.cn/enarticle/enasean/chianaseannews/200911/1473_1.html

In October 2009, Surin Pitsuwan, the then Secretary-General of ASEAN asserted that bolstering trade and economic ties with China is significant for ASEAN. Further, he posited that '*China grows, ASEAN grows*'.[31] The former Prime Minister of Laos, Bouasone Bouphavanh, stressed China's role as a key player in regional development and its inevitable help to ASEAN. Due to the FTA in January 2010, ASEAN became China's third largest trade partner by exceeding Japan. 'Companies from countries in the Association of Southeast Asian Nations (ASEAN) look to China as a key source of customers and are working to expand their presence in the world's fastest-growing major economy'.[32] Boediono, the former Vice-President of the Republic of Indonesia, noted that for ASEAN countries China has become a dependable partner and played a crucial role in numerous ventures of ASEAN.

In 2014, ASEAN expressed an interest in building the21st century Maritime Silk Road along with the green signal for ASEAN-China FTA upgradation. In the same year, Chinese Commerce Minister Gao Hucheng mentioned the need for upgradation of ACFTA. He illustrated the advantages of the upgradation. It would assist in magnifying economic cooperation. In addition, it would support the implementation of the

Maritime Silk Road Strategy and realise the China-ASEAN trade target of 1 trillion U.S. dollars in 2020 set by the leaders of both sides.[33] Henceforth, one can see the preparedness on the part of the ASEAN countries to engage with China. The bilateral trade relations are enjoying the fruits of continuous endeavours. One can describe it with the help of statistics.

ASEAN export and import vis-a-vis China

Year	*ASEAN's Exports to China (in percentage)*	*ASEAN's Imports from China (in percentage)*
2003	6.5	8.5
2013	12	16

China-Pakistan FTA

Parama Palit in her book titled *Analysing China's Soft Power Strategy and Comparative Indian Initiatives* has argued that in South Asia, China uses multiple instruments of soft power.[34] The Chinese Free Trade Agreement is one such soft power tool.

The Pakistan-China relationship is distinctive in nature. Pakistan was the third non-communist and the first Muslim country to recognise China.[35] Diplomatic relations between the two were established in 1951. The progression of China-Pakistan ties needs to be scrutinised in the context of Cold War politics in general and with the India factor in particular.

China and Pakistan are perhaps the most incongruent allies in the world. China is an atheist, authoritarian, emerging superpower; Pakistan is an Islamic, equally undemocratic, unstable, medium-sized garrison-state that in recent decades has been using Islamism, jihadism and support for terrorism to achieve its goal of becoming the dominant Islamic power in the region.[36] During the initial years of the Cold War, the USA had given arms and monetary assistance to Pakistan as an anti-communist ally and in later years against Islamic terrorism. But Pakistan used it to counter India.

The famous Pakistani political scientist, Khalid Bin Sayyad, has aptly narrated Pakistan's leaning towards China. He said that as Pakistan is surrounded by hostile neighbours such as India, Afghanistan and the Soviet Union, and has friends like the USA, Britain and other members of the Commonwealth who are far away, it has no option but to explore areas of understanding with the Communist Chinese.[37] Concurrently, the estrangement between China and the USSR and the India-China war of 1962 had drawn China closer to Pakistan. From the Chinese perspective, relations with Pakistan are of significance as Pakistan serves as a door to the Indian Ocean and the Middle East. Equation with Pakistan can help China prevent India from becoming a domineering power in South Asia.

It is a well-known fact that defence engagement is the basis of the China Pakistan relationship. China has provided nuclear technology to Pakistan in order to contain India. So, China's policy towards Pakistan was India-centric as both shared an anti-India perspective. Nevertheless, since 21st century, trade has become a vital aspect of their relationship. Therefore, it can be held that China is reinforcing its relations with Pakistan by employing the Free Trade Agreement.

Pakistan is tackling various economic hurdles. With 220 million people, 62 per cent of the population in Pakistan is dependent on agriculture. Since its independence it has been facing an internal political struggle. Pakistan has a large English-speaking population, with English-language skills less prevalent outside urban centres. Despite some progress in recent years in both security and energy, a challenging security environment, electricity shortages, and a burdensome investment climate have traditionally deterred investors. There is a lack of diversity in Pakistan's export pattern; it is merely textile and apparel oriented. Its unemployment rate is 6 per cent. Human development is unsatisfactory.[38] In such circumstances, FTA is boosting Pakistan's economy.

Furthermore, one should also understand the role of America in Pakistan to probe into the China-Pakistan relationship especially in the 21st century. Compared to Pakistan-U.S. defence trade, China's defence trade with Pakistan is quantitatively much larger which has helped Pakistan to expand its arms industry including tanks and armoured vehicles. As a result, China has emerged as a key defence partner of Pakistan. Though U.S.-Pakistan defence relations existed since the Cold War, its end brought about a change in the U.S.-Pakistan relationship resulting in the U.S. replacement by China. This is in spite of the fact that the quality of weapons and the platforms supplied by the USA have always been of a better quality than that of China. The post-World Trade Centre attacks, though the USA and Pakistan joined hands in the war against terrorism, the relations between them continue to remain partially tense because of Pakistan's alleged support to terrorist groups on the one hand and close U.S.-India relations on the other. Today, in the field of defence and security, China has exceeded the USA by becoming Pakistan's most important contributor.[39] The following tables show the volume of trade between China and Pakistan.

China's exports (goods) to Pakistan from 2008 to 2018 (US $)

Year	*Value*
2008	6.0 bn
2009	5.5 bn
2010	6.9 bn
2011	8.4 bn
2012	9.2 bn
2013	11.0 bn
2014	13.2 bn
2015	16.4 bn
2016	17.2 bn
2017	18.2 bn
2018	16.9 bn

Source: https://comtrade.un.org/data/

Pakistan's export (goods) to China in US$ from 2008 to 2018

Year	*Value*
2008	0.7 bn
2009	1 bn
2010	1.4 bn
2011	1.6 bn
2012	2.6 bn

2013	2.6 bn
2014	2.2 bn
2015	1.9 bn
2016	1.5 bn
2017	1.5 bn
2018	1.8 bn

Source: https://comtrade.un.org/

Since 2008, Pakistan's exports to China show a steady growth except from 2015 to 2018. In that period there is a slight reduction in the trend. Even so, Pakistan's approval to the second phase of FTA indicates China's strengthening of the sphere of influence. Besides, the China Pakistan Economic Corridor is the pinnacle of their relations.

The China-Pakistan FTA was signed in 2007. It led to more business opportunities and more benefits for consumers of the two countries. The bilateral trade volume has exhibited a rapid growth, groping from US$ 6.9 bn in 2007 to US$ 16 bn in 2014. The bilateral trade volume between China and Pakistan increased from US$ 5.25 bn in 2006 to US$ 19.08 bn in 2018.[40] China's exports to Pakistan are increasing slowly from 2008 to 2018.

China-Bangladesh FTA

Bangladesh is a geo-strategically important nation for India, China as well as Japan. For India, Bangladesh is a gateway to Southeast Asia and hence significant from the perspective of India's Act East Policy. For China's One Belt One Road policy Bangladesh occupies a key position. Japan has included Bangladesh in its Bay of Bengal Industrial Growth Belt (BIG-B) initiative. The increasing significance of Bangladesh and its economic growth has brought Bangladesh to the centre stage of Asia's economic set-up.[41]

The diplomatic relationship between China and Bangladesh was established in 1976. Since then, one can find consistency in their relations. After the death of Mujibur Rahman, as relations between India and

Bangladesh got strained, relations between Bangladesh and China began to improve. In 1977, the visit of General Ziaur Rahman to China led the foundation of a growing Bangladesh-China relationship which grew steadily in later years.[42] Even after the re-establishment of democracy since 1991 the relations between the two seems to remain consistent. China-Bangladesh ties are multi-dimensional in nature which incorporates defence, economic, political, and cultural aspects.

China formally proposed an FTA with Bangladesh in 2014. The memorandum of understanding (MoU) was signed in 2016 between the two countries. Now the FTA feasibility study is 'underway'. After completing all the formalities, Bangladesh will sign the FTA with China. But Bangladesh is also pursuing China to improve trade facility and increase export apparel items while seeking duty-free market access in China.[43]. Already, Bangladesh is enjoying preferential treatment from China under the APTA (Asia-Pacific Trade Agreement) and China's initiation of unilateral tariff liberalisation for least developed countries.[44]. It also enjoys duty benefits in Chinese markets. Bangladesh essentially imports machinery, cotton, consumer products and chemical products from China and it exports jute, jute products, readymade garments and processed leather to China. China is Bangladesh's biggest trading partner with bilateral trade worth US$ 10 bn dollars.[45]

Bangladesh exports (goods) to China from 2008 to 2015

Year	*Value (US dollars)*
2008	92.9 mn
2009	118 mn
2010	259 mn
2011	382 mn
2012	431 mn
2013	485 mn
2015	715 mn

Source: https://comtrade.un.org/

China's exports (goods) to Bangladesh from 2008 to 2015

Year	*Value (US dollars)*
2008	4.5 bn
2009	4.4 bn
2010	6.7 bn
2011	7.8 bn
2012	7.9 bn
2013	9.7 bn
2014	11.7 bn
2015	13.8 bn

Source: https://comtrade.un.org/

Even though the FTA has not been signed, China's exports to Bangladesh is large. It can be concluded that China is able to convert its trade relations into influence. China has taken advantage of its popularity to gain political benefit. This can be seen from the support of Bangladesh for China's entry into SAARC as an observer and Bangladesh joining the Belt and Road Initiative.

'Experts in Bangladesh and other countries are also in favour of an FTA between Bangladesh and China and also some other countries. In a theoretical study by the Centre for Policy Dialogue (CPD), an analysis was carried out to identify possible 'natural partners' for forming FTA with Bangladesh. CPD observed that countries being 'natural partners' for bilateral trade depend on mutual interest from both sides. Analysis shows that for Bangladesh, potential FTA partners could be Argentina, Brazil, Chile, China, Chinese Taipei, Malaysia, Mexico, Korea, Russia, South Africa and Ukraine'.[46]

M.S. Siddiqui has pointed out the advantages of the China-Bangladesh FTA for Bangladesh. In his opinion, there is an expansion of market for foreign goods and services in China as the country is gradually transforming into a consumption-driven, service-based economy. Bangladeshi exports to China are restricted to leather, cotton textiles, fish, etc. Due to the FTA with China, Bangladeshi exports to China would increase, new industries and firms would be established hence employment would be generated.

Consumers and manufacturers would be benefited from the import of lower-priced goods from China. China's transformation into a consumption-based economy will pave the way for greater demand for services. Bangladesh could earn more foreign currency out of this situation. The industry and service sectors in Bangladesh associated with agro-food, leather and textiles, manpower and natural resources could receive the biggest benefits from an FTA with China.[47]

China-Maldives FTA

Maldives occupies a key geostrategic position for East-West Maritime trade in the Indian Ocean. For China's increasing interest in the Indian Ocean and its need to establish its footprints in it, relationship with the Maldives become important for China. Just as the young democracy was struggling with its first political crisis, China began taking a greater interest in the Maldives. In mid-2011, at the outset of the political turmoil, Male was visited by Politburo Standing Committee (PBSC) member Wu Bangguo, the highest-ranking Chinese leader. China opened its first embassy in the Maldives in 2011. In his visit to China in 2012, President Waheed, received a pledge of $ 500 million assistance from China and a $ 150 million loan from the Export-Import Bank of China to fund a new housing complex.[48]

Yameen's election as the President of the Maldives in 2013, accelerated China-Maldives relations. He visited China in September 2014 and received a $ 16 million grant. This sum is expected to cover costs partly for the Male-Hulhule Bridge, and other projects. Beijing as a part of its aid programme, constructed a building to house the Maldives Ministry of Foreign Affairs, a national museum, and is involved in the 1,000 Housing Units Project. Additionally, Beijing is actively involved in several renewable energy projects, and tourism and telecommunication sectors.[49]

On 7 December 2017, China and the Maldives signed the FTA. It is a fresh attainment in "promoting the construction of Free Trade Areas and an open world economy". It has been stated that in terms of trade in goods, the agreed zero-tariff products and their import amount of the two sides in total account for nearly 96 per cent. Most of China's industrial products and agricultural products such as flowers, plants and vegetables exported to the Maldives will benefit from this. The Maldives' most major export products such as aquatic products will also enjoy zero tariff.[50].

Though FTA has nourished the economic relationship between the Maldives and China, experts and policy makers in the Maldives have apprehensions about it.

Chart 1: Trade Partners for the Maldives: Exports

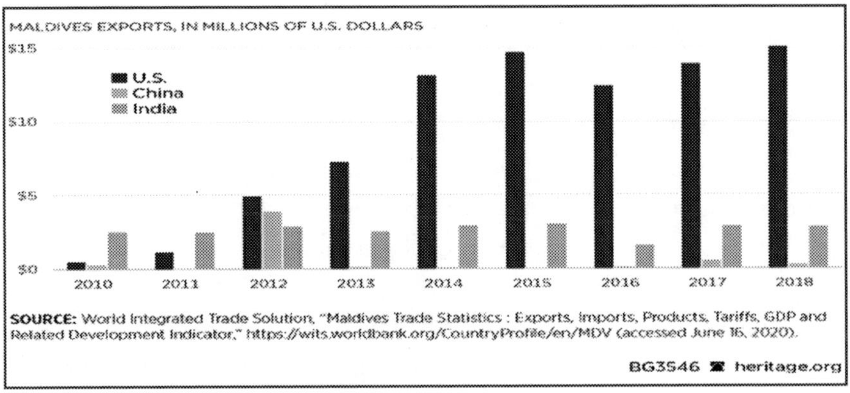

Sources: https://www.heritage.org/global-politics/report/china-and-the-maldives-lessons-the-indian-oceans-new-battleground

Chart 2: Trade Partners for the Maldives: Imports

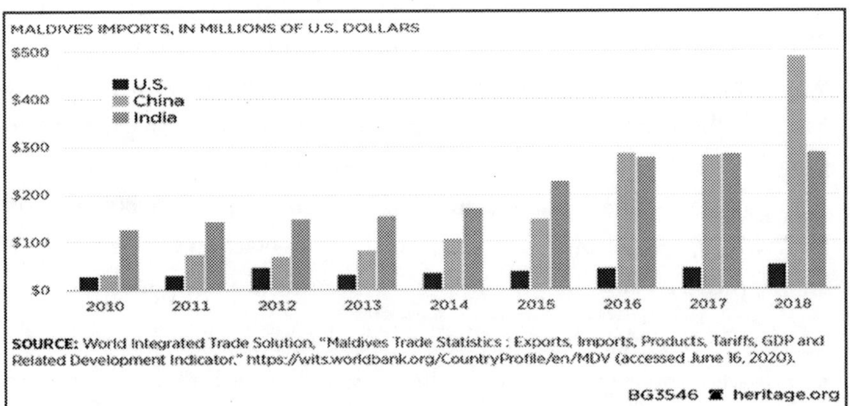

Sources: https://www.heritage.org/global-politics/report/china-and-the-maldives-lessons-the-indian-oceans-new-battleground

The above data reflects the adverse trade relationship between the Maldives and China.

Critics in the Maldives say a China-led infrastructure boom has left the tiny country of a little more than 400,000 people debt-ridden, and a free trade pact would only make the situation worse given the lopsided nature of the relationship.[51] During an interview with Indian correspondents, President of Maldives Mohamed Nasheed said that the FTA is dead. It is not proceeding and it has to come to the parliament first for it to be implemented. "And I don't see our parliamentarians having the appetite for it.[52] Hamid Abdul Ghafoor of the ruling Maldivian Democratic Party (MDP) told the *South Asian Monitor* that the MCFTA, running into 1,000 pages, was pushed through Parliament in ten minutes, giving no time for the MPs to read, understand and comment on it.[53]

The story of China's engagement with the Maldives is nevertheless instructive and offers some cause for concern. It must be viewed in the context of China's broader push into South Asia and the Indian Ocean over the past decade, where it has gained substantial ground in a region once viewed as firmly within India's sphere of influence.[54]

Conclusion

This chapter tries to examine trade as a tool of China's soft power. It has briefly discussed the evolution of Chinese economy since 1978. It has been argued that China's domestic economic progress has shaped the external economic relations. As a result, trade has occupied an important place in its foreign policy. Further, the chapter describes China's FTAs with ASEAN, Pakistan, and Bangladesh (in process) and discusses the pushback to the China-Maldives FTA.

Scholars have observed that China has adopted the gradual approach in negotiating FTAs which make other countries more dependent on China. It gives more bargaining power to China. The China-ASEAN FTA was concluded in 2004. Then China offered the 'Early Harvest' program. It allowed the reduction of tariffs on a number of ASEAN goods. Also, China had extended most favoured nation (MFN) status to new ASEAN members—Vietnam, Laos, Myanmar and Cambodia so that they could get early entry into China's market before they themselves had opened their own to Chinese competition.[55] China has nullified the loans of these new members. These concessions have portrayed China as a responsible power. In 2009, China and ASEAN had an agreement on investment. Currently, they are working on the upgradation of FTA. Despite the China-ASEAN FTA, ASEAN's trade with China is in the deficit.

The China–Pakistan FTA was concluded in 2006 and the second phase of FTA was signed in 2019. Manufacturers in Pakistan were not in support of revision of the China–Pakistan FTA. They argued that it would generate losses for local industry as they are unable to compete with their Chinese counterparts. It is to be noted that they started negotiations for the second phase in 2011. Before concluding the second phase they had eight rounds of talks in which Pakistan raised concerns about not getting meaningful market access during first phase of FTA. According to the first phase, Pakistan reduced zero per cent duty on 35 per cent of China's products and China reduced zero per cent on 40 per cent of Pakistan's products. Under the second phase, China has demanded zero per cent duty reduction on 90 per cent Pakistan's products. On the other hand, Pakistan has demanded preferential treatment which was denied by China.[56] Albeit these disagreements, Pakistan ended up with the second phase of FTA. It underlines Pakistan's dependence on China for trade. China's steady approach towards trade agreements have deepened economic links with other countries. China is enjoying a large share of their trade by becoming an export destination for these countries.

The China–Bangladesh FTA is under consideration. Both are taking benefits from the Asia Pacific Trade Agreement (APTA). Officials and experts support the China-Bangladesh FTA. They opine that Bangladesh's exports to China is low and the FTA would provide an opportunity for balanced trade.

The China-Maldives FTA faces opposition in the Maldives; nevertheless China's presence in the Maldives has not reduced. The newly-elected government in the Maldives has come to power by promising to reduce debt from China's loans. However, it has not rejected Chinese projects.

The Maldives is participating in the BRI. China is executing several housing and development projects in the Maldives. Experts believe that irrespective of who their leader is, China will work with the Maldives.

It can be argued that by enhancing the reliance of other countries on itself for trade, China is extending its sphere of influence.

NOTES

1. Overholt, W. H. (1993). *The rise of China: How economic reform is creating a new superpower.* New York: WW Norton & Company. p. 26.
2. Ibid.
3. Ibid.
4. Gittings, J. (2006). *The Changing Face of China from Mao to Market.* New York: Oxford University Press. p. 213.
5. Jacques, M. (2009). *When China rules the world: the end of the Western world and the birth of global order.* New York: The Penguin Press. p. 153.
6. Gittings, op. cit., p. 210.
7. Ibid.
8. Overholt, op. cit., p. 28.
9. Chow, G. C. (2015). *China's Economic Transformation.* UK: John Wiley & Sons. Ltd. p. 44.
10. Jacques, op. cit.,p. 153.
11. Vogel, E. F. (2011). *Deng Xiaoping and the Trasformation of China.* London: The Belknap Press of Harvard University Press. p. 394.
12. Ibid.
13. Joseph, W. A. (2014). 'Ideology and China's Political Development.' In W. A. Joseph (ed.). *Politics in China an Introduction.* New York: Oxford University Press. p. 276.
14. Zhu, X. (2012). 'Understanding China's Growth: Past, Present and Future.' *Journal of Economic Perspective,* vol..26, (November 4), pp. 103-124, https://pubs.aeaweb.org/doi/pdfplus/10.1257/jep.26.4.103, accessed on 15 April 2019.
15. Ibid.
16. Chow, G. C. (2018). 'China's Economic Transformation.' In R. Garnaut, L. Song & C. Fang (eds.). *China's 40 Years of Reforms and Development 1978-2018.* Australian National University Press, p. 94.
17. Mohanty, M. (2014). *Ideology Matters: China From Mao Zedong to Xi Jinping.* Delhi: Aakar Books. p. 97.
18. Jacques, op. cit., p. 154.
19 Joseph, op. cit., p. 268.
20. Sharma, S. D. (2009). *China and India in the age of globalisation.* New Delhi: Cambridge University Press. p. 100.
21. Fang, C. (2010). 'Labour Market Development and Expansion of Rural and Urban

Employment.' In C. Fang (ed.). *Transforming the Chinese Economy.* Netherlands: Koninklijke Brill NV. p. 88.

22. Ohashi, H. (2005). 'China's Regional Trade and Investment Prolific.' In D. Shambaugh (ed.). *Power shift China and Asia's New Dynamics*. California: University of California. p. 71.
23. Ahmed, R. (2018, May 18). 'Free Trade Agreement with China: A Necessity.' *Dhaka Tribune.* https://www.dhakatribune.com/opinion/op-ed/2018/05/18/free-trade-agreement-with-china-a-necessity, accessed on 4 August 2019.
24. International Trade Administration. (2021, February 3). 'China-Country Commercial Guide'. Retrieved from https://www.trade.gov/knowledge-product/china-trade-agreements#:~:text=China%20maintains%2016%20Free%20Trade,implementing%20an%20additional%20eight%20FTAs, accessed on 12 April 2021.
25. Saili, L.; Lee, V.; & Lin, Z. (eds.). (2013). *China's External Economic Relations.* Singapore: Enrich Professional Publishing. p. 171.
26. 'China Joins Treaty of Amity, Cooperation in Southeast Asia.' (2003, October 9). *People's Daily Online.* Retrieved from: http://en.people.cn/200310/08/eng20031008_125556.shtml, accessed on 2 August 2019.
27. Ministry of Commerce, People's Republic of China. (2006, January 24). *China-ASEAN FTA Agreement Benefits China's Textile Export.* Retrieved from http://fta.mof com.gov.cn/enarticle/enasean/chianaseannews/200911/1712_1.html, accessed on 3 August 2019.
28. Ministry of Commerce, People's Republic of China. (2007, October 31). 'China-ASEAN FTA Expected to be New Engine to Drive World Economy. Retrieved from: http://fta.mofcom.gov.cn/enarticle/enasean/chianaseannews/200911/1698_1.html, accessed on 3 August 2019.
29. Ministry of Commerce, People's Republic of China. (2008, August 30). *China-ASEAN Expo Propels FTA Construction.* Retrieved from: http://fta.mofcom.gov.cn/enarticle/enasean/chianaseannews/200911/1708_1.html, accessed on 4 August 2019.
30. Ministry of Commerce, People's Republic of China. (2009, August 19). 'ASEAN-China FTA Investment Agreement Signed'. Retrieved from http://fta.mofcom.gov.cn/enarticle/enasean/chianaseannews/200911/1473_1.html, accessed on 4 August 2019.
31. Ministry of Commerce, People's Republic of China. (2009, October 21). 'Sixth China-ASEAN Expo Opens to Embrace Free Trade Area. Retrieved from http://fta.mofcom.gov.cn/enarticle/enasean/chianaseannews/200911/1601_1.html, accessed on 4 August 2019.
32. Ministry of Commerce, People's Repiblic of China. (2010, October 22). 'ASEAN Companies Eye China for Future Growth'. Retrieved from http://fta.mofcom.gov.cn/enarticle/enasean/chianaseannews/201010/3805_1.html, accessed on 5 August 2019.
33. Ministry of Commerce, People's Republic of China. (2014, August 29). 'Interview: China, ASEAN Trade Economic Cooperation to Make New Start.' Retrieved from http://fta.mofcom.gov.cn/enarticle/enasean/chianaseannews/201411/18854_1.html, accessed on 5 August 2019.
34. Palit, P. S. (2017). *Analysing China's Soft Power Strategy and Comparative Indian*

Initiatives. New Delhi: Sage Publications India Pvt. Ltd. p. 47.

35. Kayani,F. N.;Ahmed. M.; Shah. T.A.; & Kayani, U. N. (2013). 'China-Pakistan Economic Relations: Lessons for Pakistan.' *Journal of Commerce and Social Sciences*, vol. 7(3), 454-462. Retrieved from https://papers.ssrn.com/sol3/papers.cfm?abstract_id=2892052, accessed on 2 April 2020.
36. Kemenade, W. V. (2008). *Détente Between China and India: The Delicate Balance of Geopolitics in Asia.* Netherlands Institute of International Relations, Clingendael. Retrieved from https://www.clingendael.org/sites/default/files/pdfs/20080700_cdsp_diplomacy_paper.pdf, accessed on 29 March 2020, pp. 85.
37. Sayeed, K. B. (1964). 'Pakistan's Foreign Policy: An Analysis of Pakistani Fears and Interests.' *Asian Survey*, 4(3), 746-756. Retrieved from https://www.jstor.org/stable/302356, accessed on 29 March 2020.
38. The World Factbook. (n.d.). *Pakistan.* Retrieved from https://www.cia.gov/the-world factbook/countries/pakistan/, accessed on 4 April 2020.
39. Sareen, S. (2019, February 20). 'For Pakistan, China is the New America.' Observer Research Foundation. https://www.orfonline.org/expert-speak/pakistan-china-new-america-48305/, accessed on 10 December 2019.
40. Ministry of Commerce, People's Republic of China.)2019, April 11). 'The 11th Meeting of the 2nd Phase of Negotiation of China-Pakistan FTA Makes Positive Progress.' Retrieved from http://fta.mofcom.gov.cn/enarticle/enpakistan/enpakistannews/201904/40278_1.html, accessed on 4 April 2020.
41. Bangladesh's Geopolotical Importance 'Grows'. (2017, May 29). *The Independent.* Retrieved from https://m.theindependentbd.com/printversion/details/96789, accessed 4 April 2020.
42. Bhattacharjee, J. (2018, June 27). 'Decoding China-Bangladesh Relationship.' Observer Research Foundation. Retrieved from https://www.orfonline.org/expert-speak/41935-decoding-china-bangladesh-relationship/?amp, accessed on 5 April 2020.
43. Siddiqui, M.S. (2019, March 15). 'China-Bangladesh FTA—An Overview.' *The Financial Express.* Retrieved from https://thefinancialexpress.com.bd/views/china-bangladesh-fta-an-overview-, accessed on 15 May 2019.
44. Ibid.
45. Bhattacharjee, op. cit.
46. Siddiqui, op. cit.
47. Ibid.
48. Smith, J. (2020, October 28). *China and Maldives: Lessons From the Indian Ocean's New Battleground.* The Heritage Foundation. Retrieved from https://www.heritage.org/global-politics/report/china-and-the-maldives-lessons-the-indian-oceans-new-battleground. Accessed on 15 November 2020.
49. Kondapalli, S. (2014, November 13). 'Maritime Silk Road:Increasing Chinese Inroads into Maldives.' Institute of Peace and Conflict Studies. Retrieved from http://www.ipcs.org/comm_select.php?articleNo=4735, accessed on 14 November 2020.

50. Ministry of Commerce, People's Republic of China. (2017, December 8.('China and Maldives Sign the Free Trade Agreement.' Retrieved from http://fta.mofcom.gov.cn/enarticle/chinamedfen/chinamedfennews/201712/36458_1.html, accessed on 15 Novenber 2020.
51. Miglani, S. & Junayd, M. (2018, November 19). Exclusive: 'Maldives Set to Pull Out of China Free Trade Deal, Says Senior Lawmaker.' Reuters. Retrieved from https://www.reuters.com/article/us-maldives-politics-china-exclusive-idUSKCN1NO0ZC, accessed on 15 November 2020.
52. Sibal, S. (2019, December 14). 'Maldives–China FTA ID Dead, CAB India's Internal Matter: Speaker of the Maldives Parliament.' *DNA*. Retrieved from https://www.dnaindia.com/india/report-maldives-china-fta-is-dead-cab-india-s-internal-matter-speaker-of-the-maldives-parliament-2805478, accessed on 15 November 2020.
53. Balachandran, P. K. (2019, February 8). 'Fate of Maldives–China FTA Uncertain as Male Loosens Ties with Beijing.' *bilateral.org*. Retrieved from https://www.bilaterals.org/?fate-of-maldives-china-fta, accessed on 15 November 2020.
54. Smith, op. cit.
55. Ba, A. D. (2003). 'China and ASEAN: Re-navigating Relations for 21st Century Asia.' *Asian Survey,* 43 (4), pp. 622-647. Retrieved from https://www.jstor.org/stable/10.1525/as.2003.43.4.622, accessed on 22 March 2021.
56. Khan, M. Z. (2016, July 6). 'Pakistan, China Yet to Strike Deal on FTA Phase-II.' *Dawn*. Retrieved from https://www.dawn.com/news/1269281, accessed on 10 September 2020.

Chapter Four

Investment as an Instrument of Soft Power

Introduction

China has proved herself in the field of economy and is currently in the driver's seat. It has very wisely used trade and investment for domestic economic growth and maintain favourable bilateral relations. Hence, scholars very often assert that, in recent years, China has emerged as an economic power by accomplishing its journey from a major recipient of investment to a global investor. In 2010, China's outward FDI flows were US$ 68.81 bn. After 10 years, it raised it to US$ 132.94 bn. It can be regarded as an indicator of China's expanding sphere of influence.[1]

Overview of the Evolution of China's Investment Policy

Michael Clarke, in his article titled *The Belt and Road Initiative: China's New Grand Strategy?* has elaborated extensively China's concerns and efforts in encouraging investment abroad. According to him, as economic reforms were carried out in the eastern regions of China their fruits remained centred on the same region. It led to regional economic imbalance. To address the regional disparity, the Chinese government had initiated the Great Western Development Campaign which emphasised the progress of the western provinces like Gansu, Guizhou, Qinghai, Shaanxi, Sichuan and Yunnan and autonomous regions such as Guanxi, Inner Mongolia,

Ningxia, Tibet and Xinjiang. He has argued that through the Great Western Development Campaign China was mainly trying to develop infrastructure, for example, the Xinjiang-Shanghai gas pipeline and the Qinghai-Tibet railway. Basically, Beijing had invested in infrastructure projects which would link the west to the developed east. However, there existed two challenges: firstly, absence of direct access to international markets and secondly, countries which share proximity with China's land borders like in Central Asia were considered as underdeveloped with poor governance, low infrastructure, and difficult terrain.[2]

Ma Xiuhong, the then Vice-Minister of Commerce of the PRC, has described the gradual increase in China's FDIs. She had mentioned that foreign investors from more than 192 countries and regions had set up 500,000 enterprises in China by the middle of September 2004.[3]

Besides encouraging FDIs, China was also encouraging Chinese investors to invest overseas. Beijing had formulated a policy named 'Go Out' or 'Go Global' to boost Chinese overseas investment. 'China's Ministry of Foreign Trade and Economic Cooperation selected some thirty to fifty top Chinese companies to take the lead in overseas investment. As they look to invest overseas, these national champions enjoy a range of benefits that will help them compete, including low-interest funding from Chinese banks primarily controlled by the government'.[4]

Zhan Xiaoning, a senior official on investment with UNCTAD in 2003 in an interview has illustrated the nature of China's overseas investments. He stated that China conducts different forms of outward investments, namely, resource-oriented investment means the import of some resources from abroad or exploitation of natural resources. For example, China's investments in Australia, North America, South America. The market-orientation covers the investment of many enterprises like household electric appliance enterprises such as Haier. Efficiency-oriented investment essentially includes use of cheap labour, preferential policies of host countries, for instance, China's investment in developing countries. Technology-orientation refers to the purchase of advanced technologies or brand of some enterprises from advanced countries.[5]

Belt and Road Initiative

A turning point in China's investment policy arrived in the form of 'One Belt One Road'. On 7 September 2013, at Kazakhstan's Nazarbayev University, President Xi Jinping made a speech where he proposed the idea of the 'Silk Road Economic Belt' and urged deeper cooperation between Eurasian countries. Later, in October 2013, in his speech in Indonesia, he acknowledged the flourishing relations between China and ASEAN and put forth the notion of the 'Maritime Silk Road of the 21st Century'. The 'Silk Road Economic Belt' and the 'Maritime Silk Road of the 21st Century' together were called the Belt and Road Initiative.[6]

Vision and Actions on Jointly Building Silk Road Economic Belt and 21st-Century Maritime Silk Road declared by the Chinese government on 28 March 2015 offers a systematic study of the 'One Belt One Road Initiative'. At the very beginning, the document clarifies that BRI is in compliance with the contemporary multi-polar world and aims at win-win relations. The primary objective of the initiative is to create connectivity and build infrastructure. It advocates collaboration, tolerance and respect for different models of development. It intends to cover a large geographical area by bringing together China, Central Asia, Russia and Europe (the Baltic); linking China with the Persian Gulf and the Mediterranean Sea through Central Asia and West Asia; and connecting China with Southeast Asia, South Asia and the Indian Ocean. The 21st-Century Maritime Silk Road is designed to go from China's coast to Europe through the South China Sea and the Indian Ocean in one route, and from China's coast through the South China Sea to the South Pacific in the other.[7]

The document also urges the establishment of financial mechanisms like the Asian Infrastructure Investment Bank, Silk Road Fund, China-ASEAN Interbank Association and Shanghai Cooperation Organisation Interbank Association.

Perspectives on BRI

China's announcement of the Silk Road Economic Belt and Maritime Silk Road of 21st century has generated discussions on China's foreign policy. For some, it is a geo-economic and geo-strategic policy, China's ambitious plan to create a Sino-centric Asian order and for some it is a win-win policy. Therefore, it is required to describe this discourse.

Shyam Saran, India's former Foreign Secretary, has noted the benefits of BRI for China. In his opinion it is an economic strategy. First, it would address the problem of massive overcapacity in China's industry. Second, China could utilise its unused capacity in the sector of construction material and capital equipment to create infrastructure under BRI. Third, China could export its skilled and semi-skilled labourers.[8]

Xiao Fang in his article titled '*The Belt and Road Initiative: Connecting China and Central Europe*' has underlined the role of the BRI in bolstering China and Central Europe relations wherein he has argued that BRI complements the existing economic system. It is distinctive because it transcends geographical, cultural and historical boundaries and brings a new approach of coordinating comparative advantages and advocating efficiency. The author believes that the OBOR is an attempt at regional cooperation as it can transform common features into 'motives of regional integration.[9]

Michael Clarke has examined different perceptions related to OBOR. In his opinion, the BRI is perceived in three different ways. First, to counter the USA in the Asia-Pacific and restrain the rise of America. Second, to render the economic benefits to China such as reduction of the gap between the eastern and western regions of China and channelise extensive production capacity. Third is to expand China's influence thus reflecting on the soft power narrative. In his opinion, through BRI, Beijing is trying to maintain ongoing economic growth which would provide legitimacy to the Chinese Communist Party. By creating a link between Eurasian countries, the BRI would provide an alternative to the international order. Finally, China could acquire great power status without overtly producing counter-reactions.

Another very remarkable understanding of BRI is explained by Jacob L. Shapiro in his article headed '*One Belt, One Road, No Dice*'. He has thoroughly inspected the difference between the BRI and the Marshall

Plan. He has clarified that the Marshall Plan was a highly focused and targeted set of measures formulated and executed with a clear goal in mind: to rebuild Europe so that the Iron Curtain could not spread further than it had done already across the Continent[10] whereas the '*Vision and Actions on Jointly Building Silk Road Economic Belt and 21st-Century Maritime Silk Road* document is unformed and contains only general proposals. There is an absence of an authority to supervise the execution of projects.

Like other experts, Jacob Shapiro also is of the opinion that the BRI is driven by China's domestic economic interests. It is an attempt to improve the western region of China and generate profits for Chinese provinces from infrastructural development and trade under the BRI. Further, the BRI offers access to different markets which would absorb China's surplus capacity of steel, coal and other crucial commodities.[11]

In addition, he has explained the limitations of the BRI. It has remained undefined and fighting against restraints like geography and Eurasian instability. Primarily, it is about China's domestic economic growth. Referring to the Maritime Silk Road, he has stated that there is always a possibility of militarisation in countries where China has assisted in building ports.

Nisid Hajari in his article titled '*Who Should be Afraid of One Belt One Road? China*' has argued that Xi did not invent the idea of using China's money and expertise to build infrastructure overseas. (Many projects now encompassed by the Belt and Road plan were launched long before the scheme was conceived). What he did in 2013 was to fit those efforts in a larger narrative.[12]

The study of BRI is incomplete without a discussion on the issue of the South China Sea. Damuri, Y.R., Perkasa, V., Atje, R., & Hirawan, F. in their report titled '*Perceptions and Readiness of Indonesia Towards The Belt and Road Initiative*,' have suggested that, there is an interdependece between the stability in South China Sea region and the successful implementation of BRI. On the one hand, stability in the South China Sea will enhance a mutual trust between China and ASEAN member-states and, hence stability in the region, which is necessary for a successful implementation of the BRI in Southeast Asia. A successful implementation of the BRI, on the other hand, will help improve stability in the region. Therefore, it is in the interest of all parties, China in particular, to maintain stability in the South China Sea.[13]

BRI as the Instrument of Chinese Soft Power

This section has attempted to assess the BRI in the context of the Chinese notion of soft power as explained in chapter two earlier. It observes that there are projects in different countries under the BRI such as Malaysia, Myanmar, Indonesia, Sri Lanka, Pakistan, Hungary, Greece, Kazakhstan, and Tajikistan.

Southeast Asia and China

At the outset, one can study the association between China and Southeast Asia. China's status as the world's second largest economy and the largest trading country has exerted tremendous influence on Southeast Asian economies. China's economic growth has brought enormous benefits to the region. It has taken advantage of the Sino-centric regional production created since China's admission to the World Trade Organisation in the early 2000s to export raw materials, intermediate goods, and mineral resources to China for final manufacturing into industrial goods before their export to major consumption markets in the West.[14]

Southeast Asian countries occupy a significant position in the BRI due to their geostrategic location. Hence, they are capable of making it a successful strategy. Besides, they might receive vast benefits from the BRI. For instance, domestic companies in trade, finance, shipping, aviation and information and communication technology can make profits under BRI. Moreover, to improve the inter-regional connectivity, China has promised to provide financial resources to construct large-scale transportation projects. It highlights China's attempts to strengthen trade, investment, and infrastructure links with Southeast Asia. The Singapore-Kunming Rail Link could be a representative example of infrastructural investment by China which would facilitate trade and investment in Southeast Asia.

Malaysia

Vital projects that are covered under BRI in Malaysia include the East Coast Rail Link (ECRL), Malaysia-China Kuantan Industrial Park (MCKIP), Malacca Gateway National Maritime Park, and Iskandar Malaysia Development.[15]

As BRI incorporates the building of industrial parks, agricultural farms, railways, airport, roads, and fibre-optic networks, it would result in the overall development of the hinterland in Malaysia.[16] Therefore, a project like MCKIP will provide a big steel industry near Kuantan Port, which will give the seaport more cargo to handle.[17] Gradually, Malaysian seaport capacity could be enhanced to cater to the needs of increased cargos. At present, seaport hinterland connectivity in Malaysia is dependent only on roads. BRI can provide railway links from ports to the hinterland such as the East Coast Rail Link (ECRL) which aims to connect the eastern coast of Malaysia with the western part of the country.[18] ECRL will enable the flow of oil and other commodities from the Middle East to China thereby avoiding the Strait of Malacca. Against this background, the project seems not just a solid investment but also a stroke of strategic genius.[19]

In the 2018 elections, a new coalition government led by Pakatan Harapan (PH) came to power. The new government raised a lot of questions about ECRL, about its financing, lop-sided deal, and even possible corruption.[20] Nisid Hazari has analyzed ECRL critically. In his opinion, few citizens of Malaysia will possibly appreciate the route. However, it might not be liked by shipping companies as they will have to pay more for saving merely 30 hours of transportation. But later, the Malaysian government gave the green signal to all projects under BRI with the recommendation for re-negotiations.

One can find the reasons for which Malaysia has maintained a positive stand on BRI. According to Parameswaran P., China remains a top trade and investment partner and a major player in the Malaysian economy despite some concerns about aspects of Beijing's behaviour as it was the more specific tradeoffs inherent in the deal itself. Most notably, Malaysia had had to contend with the fact that nixing the project would mean that it would be liable to pay the associated cancellation costs in the context of the country's ever-increasing debt levels.[21]

One needs to understand the fact that the Malaysian government has never abandoned the concept of BRI. It perceived it as an opportunity to ameliorate the country's infrastructure. With the help of Digital BRI, Green BRI, and Health Silk Road, Malaysia can improve some sectors. In an interview with Mercy Kuo, Chow Bing Ngeow, director of the Institute of China Studies at the University of Malaya in Kuala Lumpur, Malaysia, said, "*The challenges lie in the implementation of the BRI vision, namely how the individual projects were negotiated and executed.*"[22] He has further suggested that countries need to be well prepared to negotiate on BRI projects so as to attain benefits for their economic growth.

On the other hand, China has acknowledged that the new government requires re-assessment of relations from China's side. By aligning with Malaysia, China has sent the message that it is open for discussion on any issues related to BRI projects.

Myanmar

Myanmar offers an interesting case study for BRI. China regards Myanmar as a 'land bridge' to reach the Indian Ocean and China is dependent on Myanmar to fulfil its energy demand as gas and oil are the biggest components of Myanmar's export box. As a result, Myanmar plays a crucial role in BRI. It joined the BRI in 2017 at the Belt and Road Forum for International Cooperation. Major projects of BRI in Myanmar are China-Myanmar Economic Corridor (CMEC), Kyaukphyu Deep Sea Port Project, Myitsone Project, New Yangon Development Project and Kyaukphyu-Kunming Railway. These projects will deliver infrastructure, construction, manufacturing, agriculture, transport, finance, human resources development, telecommunications, and research and technology.[23]

It has been observed that China has taken advantage of the Rohingya issue to expand its influence in Myanmar. On one hand, Western countries were drifting away from Myanmar because of its mishandling of the Rohingya crisis; on the other, China was coming closer to it. China has acted as a peace broker between the government and ethnic groups. Also, it had off-the-record meetings with leaders from parliament, government, and the armed forces. Sun Guoxiang, Chinese Special Envoy sent to the Myanmar-Bangladesh Border offered to mediate a diplomatic row between Bangladesh and Myanmar over the flight of the minority Rohingya Muslims, who have faced persecution from Arakanese Buddhists and the military.[24] Meanwhile both the countries were working on BRI. CMEC was proposed as a BRI project during the same time.

At the time of Aung San Suu Kyi, BRI projects were under scrutiny. The Kyaukphyu Deep Sea Port Project of US$ 10 bn aims to develop a new deep sea port and industrial park. It has received objections from government officials and experts. They have debt fears and have suggested to minimise the scale of the project. To link China's Yunan province to the Indian Ocean, it was decided to build the Kyaukpyu-Kunming Railway. It has raised concerns owing to social opposition, financial feasibility, distribution of gains and national security.[25]

The current military Junta is reviewing all projects optimistically. A month after the coup, the military regime allegedly reorganised the leading committees charged with implementing the projects of BRI.[26] In May 2021, the rulers had re-arranged the management committee for the Kyaukphyu Special Economic Zone which has an authority to implement the Special Economic Zone and the deep sea port project. They approved small infrastructure projects under CMEC. The Junta has assured China about the execution of BRI projects. Now the ball is in China's court. Myanmar is experiencing post-coup chaos. Already anti-Chinese sentiments existed due to the social and environmental impact of BRI projects. For example, 10,000 villagers in Kachin state were displaced due to the suspended Myitsone dam; protests were made in Rakhine state and people demanded fair compensation from Chinese SOEs. China's support to the coup and military rule will further hamper China's presence in Myanmar.

It is believed that China does not have any alternative but to carry out its business with Myanmar. Zhao, a member of a Chinese think tank said, "*Myanmar is strategically important and a friendly neighbour to China. When others shun (Myanmar) due to its political crisis, Chinese companies will step in.*"[27] During a special meeting of ASEAN-China foreign ministers, the Chinese Foreign Minister asserted that irrespective of Myanmar's internal and external conditions, China will implement bilateral projects.

Experts recommend that China can channelise the peace process to avoid displeasure from Myanmar in particular and from other Southeast Asian countries in general. It can manoeuvre Tatmadaw to implement the Five-Point ASEAN Consensus. It can use some creative measures with the help of ASEAN to convince Tatmadaw to surrender power, etc. If China desires to maintain its hold in the region, it must avoid the trap the Tatmadaw set to cause China to view the coup solely through the prism of geo-political competition—a perspective that disregards Myanmar's internal realities.[28]

Indonesia

The announcement of the '21st century Maritime Silk Road' in Jakarta explains the significance of Indonesia for China in the BRI. China has been playing the role of a financial supporter since the re-calibration of its relations with Indonesia in 1990 such as providing a line of credit during the Asian financial crisis, and rendering soft loans for infrastructure development. Nonetheless, BRI projects can be considered as landmarks in their relations.

It has been examined that Indonesia does not have a well-developed, well-articulated and coherent trade strategy.[29] Indonesia has always developed a mixed perspective towards trade. Many Indonesians are positive about exports while some, especially Indonesian producers, believe that the domestic market is sufficient to absorb their products. Furthermore, there is little competitiveness which prevents Indonesia from becoming a major global player. Low competitiveness of the country is because of the relatively low human capital, and absence of quality infrastructure.

The BRI offers an alternative source of financing for the development of infrastructure in Indonesia. During the Belt and Road Forum for International Conference 2017, Indonesian President Joko Widodo had recollected the objective of the BRI to boost regional, sub-regional and inter-regional integration by creating roads, railways, and ports. Moreover, China's BRI is in compliance with Indonesia's 'Global Maritime Fulcrum' whose goal is to facilitate maritime infrastructure.[30]

The Jakarta-Bandung High Speed Rail Project is a landmark element in BRI. It would minimise the travelling time from three hours to 40 minutes. It has received a USD 6 bn loan from China. Later, the Indonesian government has realised the financial risks involved in the project. Hence, President Jokowi had ordered the Coordinating Minister for Maritime Affairs, and the Minister of SOE, to discover ways to lower Indonesian shares in the project from 60 per cent to just 10 per cent.[31]

There are various problems associated with BRI in Indonesia like overflow of Chinese workers. ISEAS Yusof Ishak Institute, Singapore, has undertaken a national survey according to which about 50.2 per cent of the participants are of the opinion that a limited number of Chinese workers should be permitted to work in Indonesia. Around 26.6 per cent oppose the policy that allows Chinese workers to work in Indonesia and 19.9 per cent respondents say that only highly skilled Chinese workers should be allowed to work in Indonesia. In the field research carried out by CSIS in North Sulawesi and North Sumatera, the respondents are of the opinion that foreign investment, including Chinese investment, should generate as many jobs as possible for Indonesians as Indonesia has a sufficient workforce for low-skill, non-managerial jobs.[32]

There persist two opposite perspectives about China among Indonesians. On the one hand, they appreciate China, probably because of its rapid emergence as a global economic and military power, and on the other, there is a suspicion or distrust towards Chinese investment, including BRI, as well as social-cultural initiatives. The opposition has used the issue of Chinese migrant workers to create public opinion against President Jokowi.

Meanwhile, a few experts have advised that the interests of Muslims in the country should be the government's priority. Indonesia has been wary of concerns about ongoing BRI projects but has remained open to ways to address how to manage opportunities and challenges with China.[33] Therefore, it is claimed that, the successful implementation of BRI will depend also on the government's ability to deal with such issues. Dialogues among different interest groups on current government policy towards the BRI can be encouraged so that misperceptions and mistrust about the government's intent can be avoided.

South Asia and China

The following factors need attention with respect to China-South Asia relations. First, China is relatively a 'newcomer' in the region. Second, except for India, it does not have bitter relations with any other South Asian country. Third, China shares border with four South Asian countries—Bhutan, India, Nepal and Pakistan. Finally, China is deepening its foothold in South Asia with economic engagement.

Parama Sinha Palit in her book titled '*Analysing China's Soft Power Strategy and Comparative Indian Initiatives*' has mentioned the roots of China-South Asia relations. She has mentioned that China's link with South Asia is mainly stimulated by the 'Western Development Strategy' (WDS). WDS was to uplift China's backward western region by linking it to new markets and economic hubs on its west along with getting access to energy resources and building roads, and seaport facilities in South Asia.[34] She has also pointed out that due to their geo-strategic location in the Indian Ocean, the Maldives and Sri Lanka have received significance in China's foreign policy. It has been observed that, Beijing wields a finely tailored approach towards each country'[35] in South Asia and especially during the Xi Jinping regime. China has expanded engagement with the region in multiple realms such as trade, investment, culture and higher education and its swiftly making inroads into the region by harnessing its seductive economic largesse.[36]

Pakistan

The China-Pakistan Economic Corridor (CPEC) is a highly discussed element of the BRI. In general, it is a collection of projects in sectors in transport such as road and rail links, energy such as oil and gas pipelines, fibre optics, dams, ports, airports, and special economic zones that link China's western city of Kashgar to the Gwadar port of Balochistan.[37] It officially began in 2015.

Many scholars have narrated the lucrative benefits which China will receive from the CPEC. The Corridor will facilitate the transport of huge quantity of goods from China to Africa, Europe and the Middle East via Gwadar port. It will reduce the distance and time of shipping. With the construction of oil and gas pipelines, China will meet its energy needs. The Corridor will become a link between South Asia and East Asia as well as the Gulf and the Middle East. China will have a direct route to the Indian Ocean. Wealthy Pakistan implies the absence of extremism. Economically and militarily stronger, Pakistan can compete with India and last but not least China can possibly take steps towards the internationalisation of renminbi.

M.S. Pratihibha in her article named '*China-Pakistan Economic Corridor*' has argued that the idea of the CPEC is driven by China's geo-strategic interests. China wishes to maintain the status of an economically domineering power so that it can prepare norms to its own advantage and exert influence. Therefore, China pursues such ideas that could combine its economic power and shrink its strategic weaknesses. Pakistan's constant push for Chinese investment and interest in Gwadar port for many years offered an opportunity to realise its aspirations. In return, China has raised expectations in Pakistan that the CPEC is a 'game-changer' that could not only provide Pakistan with capital and mend infrastructure but also offer a chance to compete with India's economic power.[38]

One of the objectives of BRI is to promote regional integration. The CPEC as a core project of the BRI will offer an opportunity for China and Pakistan to deepen their ties instead of only focusing on regional geo-politics. It is stated that the future of other BRI projects is dependent on proper execution of CPEC.

Mario Esteban has assessed the CPEC from three angles—first, a transit corridor, second, an economic corridor and third, a development corridor. In his opinion, CPEC offers an exceptional opportunity to Pakistan for tackling some of the main barriers hindering its economic development: energy bottlenecks, poor connectivity, and limited attraction for foreign investors.[39]

Under the proposed project, a high-speed railway track will be constructed from Karachi to Peshawar at a cost of $ 2.8 bn. Punjab province has the largest population in Pakistan. The China-Pakistan Corridor has a number of projects in Punjab province, including highways, power stations, rail transportation and other projects. The China-Pakistan Economic Corridor is not only one road or railway track but would generate economic activities, jobs, and many industries such as tourism, port facilities, transportation services, solar energy, wind energy, beach industry, renewable energy, ship building, and Oil and Gas exploration; these are feasible for investors in Baluchistan.[40]

Feng, D. in his article '*BRI a Cornerstone for Growth in Pakistan*' admires the progress achieved in the implementation of three-dozen-plus projects as part of the early harvest phase–I (2015-2020). He has mentioned the opinion of Muhammad Zamir Assad, a journalist from *Independent News*. Muhammad Zamir Assad has highlighted the benefits of CPEC availed by Pakistan. He stated that it has helped in addressing the issue of power shortage in the country. The Orange Line Metro Line, Pakistan's electric powered public transport project is complete. Nearly 70,000 direct jobs have been generated.[41]

Experts have illustrated the obstacles in the execution of CPEC. Muhammad Arshad and Zhao Haidong have elaborated on the social composition of Pakistan and asserted that lack of national unity has become an obstacle in realisation of the CPEC. Pakistan's four provinces, Punjab, Sindh, Balochistan and Khyber Pakhtunkhwa, respectively, have their own ethnic majorities. Each ethnic group has a different language, culture, and living style.

Lack of ethnic structure of the ethnic group is overwhelmingly dominant and not conducive to the formation of a national identity;

religious groups claim national identity on the basis of religious foundation. Security forces, the Government of Pakistan, and educational institutes have failed to effectively solve issues between different ethnic groups because they do not agree with one other. Since there is no agreement on which area the Corridor will be first constructed in Pakistan, so consensus on the subject is difficult. The national problem is mostly fundamental reason and Pakistan has no real national political party.[42] Local insurgent groups in Balochistan are against the CPEC because they do not receive any economic benefit.

Grant Farr has elucidated domestic issues as an impediment in the CPEC. He has pointed out that political leaders in Pakistan are supportive of it believing it may bring economic benefits to Pakistan that may not be reflected in economic prosperity for the common people. A high level of corruption and a rigid class system can prove to be a major obstacle in reaching wealth to the common population. It seems the CPEC will enhance the gap between the rich and the poor. The employment generated by CPEC will primarily benefit the Chinese and Pakistani locals will continue with lower rank services such as cleaners, guards, or assembly workers.

It is argued that the project will trigger a class conflict in Pakistan. Pakistan is essentially a rural society with 66 per cent of the population living in the countryside. There is increasing unrest in these rural areas. They believe that they are treated unequally by Islamabad. The rural population will not earn any profit from the CPEC since most of the investments are centred on cities or wealthier areas.[43]

The CPEC will link Pakistan's Southern Gwadar port (626 kilometres, 389 miles, west of Karachi) in Balochistan on the Arabian Sea to China's western Xinjiang region.[44] Hence, Balochistan has become an integral part of the CPEC. There is a growing demand for the creation of a separate state of Balochistan. Baloch nationals are against the CPEC as it will badly affect the demography of Balochistan. They are worried about the migration of people from other ethnic groups to Balochistan. There are incidents of kidnapping and killing of Chinese citizens by Baloch militants.

Militant groups are another challenge for the CPEC in Pakistan. The threat emanating from fundamentalist Islamic groups is more serious as China does not carry a good image in the Islamic world. China's non-tolerant approach towards Muslim groups within China, mainly its treatment of the Uygur in Xinjiang province, has resulted in tensions with respect to the security of the CPEC project.

The real question is, then, will the CPEC help or hinder Pakistan moving forward. On the one hand, the $ 60 bn investment will bring resources to Pakistan. Pakistan can certainly use better roads and an updated and efficient railway system, and the project may help modernise Pakistan's traditional, outdated, and very inefficient agricultural system. However, it is now becoming clear that the CPEC is hindered by the very nature of Pakistani society, particularly the provincial tensions and the lack of effective leadership in Islamabad.[45]

To conclude, through the CPEC, China is fulfilling its own national interests such as to encircle India, to satisfy its energy needs, and obtaining alternative routes to the Strait of Malacca. Pakistan is facing numerous domestic issues and also worries about increasing debts. However, it has been observed that elites in Pakistan are in support of the project but the common people are hesitant towards CPEC.

Sri Lanka

Sri Lanka, a country in the Indian Ocean Region (IOR) is highly discussed as an example of China's debt diplomacy. For more than 25 years, Sri Lanka had suffered from a civil war. As a consequence, its infrastructure has remained impoverished. During the last years of the civil war, Mahindra Rajapaksa became the President of Sri Lanka. The international community was criticising Sri Lanka on account of human rights abuses. China had extended economic and defence aid throughout the civil war and continued to support Sri Lanka in the field of security and infrastructure development even after the end of the civil war. It is obvious for a country like Sri Lanka to participate in the BRI considering its need for economic progress which has been halted due to a prolonged civil war.

Anshu Chatterjee has made an in-depth analysis of Sri Lanka's maritime strategy and has provided an interesting analysis for Sri Lanka's acceptance of BRI. In his opinion, it would cater to Sri Lanka's maritime interests. Immediately after the declaration of BRI, Sri Lanka has presented its maritime strategy. The island's proximity to the busy Sea Lines of Communication (SLOC's) provides Sri Lanka with an opportunity to grow its blue economy. This opportunity is a double-edged sword as increased traffic in its sea lanes produces a need for furthering its security in its economic exclusion zones which have seen a rise in illicit activities associated with drug transportation and threats to fisheries.[46] China's early presence at Sri Lankan port as a security and infrastructure provider made Sri Lanka a perfect prospect to realise a win-win policy—an essential objective of BRI.

When it was decided to build a port in Hambantota, officials had questioned its viability because Colombo already had a flourishing port. The feasibility studies also indicated its impracticality. Hambantota was inaugurated in 2010 with the Exim Bank of China giving US$ 306.7 million as loan but it could not generate profits as ships were using the Colombo Port. For example, in 2012, Hambantota accommodated only 34 ships whereas Colombo berthed 3,667 ships. It was Rajapaksa who pushed the deal ahead. He asked for US$ 757 million from the Chinese government in 2012. On account of increasing debt and the port's cost, the opposition party raised doubts about China's intentions. After the announcement of BRI, the Hambantota Port Project got assimilated under BRI.

In the final months of Sri Lanka's 2015 election, China's ambassador broke with diplomatic norms and lobbied voters, even caddies at Colombo's premier golf course, to support Mr. Rajapaksa against the opposition, which was threatening to tear up economic agreements with the Chinese government.[47] China sponsored the elections with huge amounts. During the 2015 Sri Lankan elections, large payments from the Chinese port construction fund flowed directly to campaign aides and activities for Rajapaksa, who had agreed to Chinese terms at every turn and was seen as an important ally in China's efforts to tilt influence away from India in South Asia.[48]

Rajapaksa lost the elections. The newly-elected government, under the leadership of President Maithripala Sirisena, had decided to scrutinise Sri Lanka's financial deals. It became impossible for Sri Lanka to pay back loans it had borrowed to build the project. Hence, Sri Lanka had to lease the port to China for 99 years. It is stated that China has used debt trap diplomacy to extend its sphere of influence in Sri Lanka.

The example of Hambantota is used to depict China's BRI as an abhorrent project. The prevailing view is Sri Lanka was forced to surrender Hambantota port to China due to its incapacity to repay the loan. Some consider it as interference in the country's sovereignty. Also, critics don't find any economic viability of the port. Some scholars uphold the opposite opinion and they defend China. They point out that Sri Lanka's debt to China is no higher than its debt to some other countries and multilateral development banks.[49] Besides Hambantota there are other ongoing projects in Sri Lanka operating under BRI such as CICT Colombo port terminal, Colombo Lotus Tower-Telecommunication Tower, Matala airport, Lakvijaya power plant, etc. Many professionals in fact opine that they are beneficial for Sri Lanka.

The daily *Financial Times* has described the opinions gathered from selected professionals from Sri Lanka to understand the perception of China's BRI and investments in Sri Lanka. According to Dr. Palitha Kohana, Sri Lanka's ambassador to China, BRI is an opportunity and leaders and officials in Sri Lanka have welcomed it. Against this backdrop of COVID-19, it is an answer to the economic problems faced by developing and underdeveloped countries. Prof. Samitha Hetige, civil educator and broadcaster, has argued that people in Sri Lanka should support BRI projects to make their lives better. They should not come under the influence of those who do not want Sri Lanka's progress. Asela Waidyalankara, a technology professional, has proposed that technology collaborations between Sri Lanka and China should be facilitated through the 'Digital Silk Road'.[50]

It has been observed that Sri Lanka has all-inclusive environmental regulations although lacking in their proper implementation and it does not possess data on inbound migration which leads to illegal migration. Researchers have commented that instead of just discussing debt trap diplomacy, Sri Lanka should consider the environmental and labour impacts of Chinese investment to ensure they get the most out of the BRI.[51]

Europe and China

The less discussed but essential component of BRI is its European end. China's growing presence in Europe is evident through the participation of European Union member-countries in BRI. Till now two-thirds of the EU members have signed up for BRI. China has cautiously selected nodal points along the land corridor and terminal points along the maritime corridor to create its influence on the eastern and western sides of Eurasia.[52] Notable BRI investments are in Hungary—the Budapest-Belgrade Railway—and Greece, the Piraeus port.

Hungary's positioning as an Eastern European country gives it the advantage of cheaper labour and a geographical location closer to Beijing, while its Western identity gives it access to the single market the Chinese desire.[53] The Budapest-Belgrade Railway, the Hungarian section of BRI, would allow Hungary to be a centre for European logistical networks as Chinese goods travel from Greece to western Europe.[54] A loan agreement was signed between China and Hungary to provide money for the building of a railway link between Budapest and Belgrade. Eighty-five per cent of the amount will be given by China as a loan and the remaining 15 per cent will be from Hungary. It is stated that Hungary's policy on Eastern Opening[55] is in synergy with BRI. Hungary practices the concept of a workforce society. This implies low taxes, reasonable regulations, highly trained workers and a favourable investment environment.[56] Therefore, Hungarian Prime Minister Viktor Orban is of the opinion that his country is an ideal pillar of BRI.

Another remarkable BRI project is the Piraeus port of Greece. China has leveraged the situation of the Greek economic crisis and secured its presence at the port of Piraeus. It will serve as a major logistics hub for Chinese trade with Europe.[57] Since 2009 China has been handling Piraeus port and has spent 600 million Euros to improve its infrastructure and equipment. Under a 2016 Greek privatisation agreement, COSCO Shipping bought a 51 per cent holding in the Piraeus Port Authority (PPA) for 280 million Euros ($ 341 million) and committed to mandatory investments worth about 300 million Euros over five years to acquire an additional 16 per cent stake.[58] There was opposition to COSCO's expansion in 2020 in the form of its 16 per cent additional stake. Though it is getting delayed, China is optimistic about the agreement and even Greek officials advocate communication and cooperation on the matter. In addition, the port of Rotterdam, is reckoned as a logistics centre for China-Europe trade. China has also established a logistics and transport hub at Wigan (Manchester) and Schiphol airport in Amsterdam.

China emphasises on financial integration among countries through BRI. The UK has occupied an important place towards that direction. China is promoting Renminbi internationalisation, formulation of the Yuan bond market and expansion of Chinese banking in the UK. Several British banks are allowed to operate in China with licences. It could be stated that China-Europe relations are facilitating supply chains and financial networks through BRI.

Central Asia and China

The Central Asian Region consists of Kazakhstan, Kyrgyzstan, Tajikistan, Turkmenistan and Uzbekistan. Amongst these, Kazakhstan, Tajikistan and Kyrgyzstan are contiguous with China. Assel Bitabarova in an article titled '*Unpacking Sino-Central Asian Engagement along the New Silk Road: A Case Study of Kazakhstan*' has indicated three factors which can be considered as drivers in China's thinking on Central Asia in general and Central Asia's place in BRI in particular. The first is Central Asia's geostrategic location, particularly its proximity with Xinjiang—China's largest administrative unit with ethnic complex. Beijing wishes for stable external environment to safeguard the security and economic growth of Xinjiang. The second is Russia's presence. China has realised Russia's special standing in Central Asia. The creation of the Eurasian Economic Union is perceived as Russia's dominance in the region. Russia impeded China's initiatives to form a Regional Development Bank or Anti-Crisis Fund. Russia is fully aware of China's strong economic position. The third is to acquire the hydrocarbon resources of Central Asia for its ever-increasing energy needs.[59]

Besides, there are other factors like the insufficiency of Shanghai Cooperation Organisation (SCO) to fulfil China's economic interests, problems in the South China Sea and the USA's efforts to prevent China in the Asia-Pacific which underscore the significance of the inland corridors of the region. One can have a glance at a few BRI projects in Central Asian countries.

Kazakhstan

Kazakhstan has been using metaphorical Silk Road to express its historical links with China and always sees itself as a cornerstone of the modern Silk Road. Eventually it is playing the role of a 'trailblazer' in shaping contours and 'stuffing-up' the obscure New Silk Road proposal with concrete measures and a timeframe in the region.[60] Taking into account its vast territory, stable political environment, favourable investment milieu and closeness with Russia it has become a key facilitator in BRI. Moreover, Kazakhstan's '*Nurly Zhol*'[61] program which aims at infrastructure development is compatible to China's BRI.

One of China's the most ambitious BRI projects in Kazakhstan is the Khorgos Gateway. The Khorgos trans-shipment hub, a so-called dry port, lies close to the border with China and is important because the two countries have different rail gauges. Here, cranes load Chinese rail freight onto Kazakh trains bound for Western European markets.[62] Beyond the logistics hub, the Kazakh project also consists of a special economic zone to attract investors to build factories and warehouses, and a free-trade border zone that aims to increase commerce with China. On the Kazakh side of the border, a purpose-built village, Nurkent, houses the area's workers, with ambitious plans to grow it in the coming decades to complement its sister city in China, also called Khorgos, which already features shopping malls, hotels, and a population of more than 100,000.[63]

Officials in Kazakhstan are enthusiastic about the project. They are hopeful about the positive outcome of the BRI initiative. They point out the country's capacity to progress. A study conducted by the International Union of Railways in 2017 showed that trade between China and Europe via rail would grow drastically in the next decade making Kazakhstan a crucial junction.

However, Yigal Chazan in his article titled '*China BRI Ventures Run into Trouble in Kazakhstan*' has argued that people have doubts about the economic viability of the Khorgos project. It has been revealed that China has subsidised rail shipments which led to the running of empty freight cars to and from Western Europe. Further, it is observed that the rail route is faster but expensive. One more project of BRI is the light railway scheme in its capital, Nur-Sultan, which was supposed to be completed by 2017 but remained unfinished. In 2018, China halted finances to the of 22-km network due to the breakdown of the local bank holding its finances. Then, in 2019, it was decided to borrow money from domestic sources to accomplish the project but, the President ordered an inquiry of the officials involved in the project.

Kazakhs have argued that only Chinese labourers and Chinese contractors are used for various projects and as a result local people remain jobless and local elites become rich. Apart from these problems, Kazakhs have carried out demonstrations against Chinese projects due to prosecution of Muslims in China's Xinjiang province. It was estimated that 1.5 million local Uighurs and ethnic Kazakhs were targeted.

Tajikistan

Tajikistan is one of the firm supporters in the Belt and Road initiative, which was known as its first signatory of an MoU with China on the Silk Road Economic Belt.[64] The BRI project here is already in service. The Dushanbe-2 thermal power station completed in 2016 provides 60 per cent of the power required by the Tajik capital, Dushanbe, as well as for restarting central heating for more than 700,000 local residents after a 15-years gap. 'The Vahdat-Yavan Railway has been completed along with bridges and tunnels, connecting the previously separated railways in southern and northern Tajikistan'.[65]

BRI projects in Tajikistan are facing challenges primarily due to domestic factors. In Tajikistan, it is not compulsory to hire local labour. As a result, Chinese companies recruit mostly Chinese workers. Such policies are not generating jobs for local people and enhancing reliance on outside support. The Tajikistan government does not pay back loans to the bank and instead relinquishes land and mining rights. China has completed a power plant in Dushanbe in 2016; in return, President Emomali Rahmon accorded a licence to the Chinese contracting company, Tebian Electric Apparatus (TBEA), to operate two gold mines. TBEA will operate these mines until it recovers the cost of the power plant.

In this scenario, China is using its own companies and workers to construct projects and then extract resources. Tajikistan is being deprived from economic benefits. Chinese loans are adding to the regime's corruption and human rights abuses.

Three BRI corridors intersect in Tajikistan. The Tajikistan-China-Mongolia-Russia, Land Bridge Economic Corridor and China-Central Asia-West Asia Economic Corridor. Properly placed to provide leverage to China, it is an essential country for BRI execution. For the benefits of the BRI to trickle down to the people of Tajikistan, it is suggested that Chinese construction and mining operations should be subjected to a local labour quota. The Tajikistan government should use Chinese grants to build schools and hospitals.

There is a mix of opinions about BRI in Central Asian countries. Advocates of the initiative argue that implementation of BRI will stimulate economies of Central Asian countries. Chinese investment will boost the emergence of new industrial, transport and communication and other facilities, and new jobs in the region. Central Asia will become a huge transport corridor linking China with the outside world.

Those who oppose the initiative claim that its implementation will lead to China's greater economic presence in the region, which can result in its political domination. They emphasise that Chinese companies that are agents of the Chinese government already control the key sectors of the national economies of the region, for example, the oil and gas industry in Kazakhstan and the mining industry in Tajikistan. They assert that the BRI's insistence on the rapid creation of new jobs for local people, associated with its implementation, are baseless. In reality, Chinese companies generate jobs in Central Asia only for Chinese citizens.

Conclusion

This chapter analyses investment as a tool of China's soft power. It revolves particularly around China's investment in infrastructure development. It has discussed connectivity projects in Southeast Asia, South Asia, Europe and Central Asia.

The official document on China's Vision and Actions on jointly building the Silk Road Economic Belt and the 21st Century Maritime Silk Road could be deemed as a narrative of China's soft power. According to the document, the BRI embraces current trends like a multi-polar world, economic globalisation, cultural diversity and greater IT application. It underscores China's commitment to deepen mutually beneficial cooperation with Asia, Europe, Africa and the rest of the world. More importantly, it shows China's readiness to shoulder responsibilities and obligations in promoting peace and the development of human beings.[66]

China concentrates on international transport facilitation by building road and railway networks and port infrastructure. Besides, China advocates financial integration through the Asian Infrastructure Investment Bank (AIIB), BRICS New Development Bank and the Silk Road Fund. Further, it encourages people-to-people communications and cultural exchanges. Finally, China has assured that BRI is inclusive in nature and that participation of all countries and organisations is welcome. By convincing others that China will work with BRI countries in the development of human and material resources, it has subtly commanded legitimacy. Throughout the document it has been assured that countries will not work for China but they will work in collaboration. Hitherto, 140 countries have participated in BRI which indicates the popularity of the project.

Southeast Asian countries possess inadequate infrastructure and consider BRI as an opportunity for the betterment of connectivity. In the case of South Asia, except for India, other South Asian countries look at China's presence as advancing their national interests. Countries here are also concerned about India's dominance in the region. Hence, they are inclined towards China as an alternative. South Asian countries face infrastructure deficiency. They are lacking in better roads, ports, telecommunication networks and electricity. Not all EU countries support BRI but Hungary and Greece, both BRI beneficiaries, acted as a bloc when the EU tried to criticise China. Central Asian countries do not have direct access to oceans and shipping routes; they also lack transportation infrastructure. BRI could facilitate inter and intra transportation. It would reduce the financial burden on local governments. It can generate jobs and thereby increase the tax revenue of Central Asian countries which can be further utilised for social development.

The current pandemic is indeed a litmus test for the BRI. One needs to understand that one of the reasons for which China has initiated BRI is to realise unimpeded domestic economic growth. COVID-19 has placed a brake on China's speedy progress. Some experts opine that it is BRI which possibly can assist China in sustaining long-term economic growth of BRI participants (mostly developing and underdeveloped countries) facing challenges due to COVID-19. However, the second largest economy in the world, China, is in a better position and still can extend help to BRI countries.

In this context, China is using the Health Silk Road (injected into BRI in 2017) to develop the health infrastructure of BRI countries. For example, China has supplied testing kits, masks, and medical supplies to Pakistan, Sri Lanka and Bangladesh. It would probably help to maintain a positive image of China.

China did maintain secrecy in disclosing the information on the corona virus. There was a possibility of discontent towards China amongst BRI countries but, we have not witnessed any major discomfort against China. This factor underlines the charm associated with BRI.

NOTES

1. 'Annual Outflow of Foreign Direct Investment (FDI) from China between 2010 and 2020'. (n.d.). *Statista.* Retrieved from https://www.statista.com/statistics/858019/china-outward-foreign-direct-investment-flows/, accessed on 15 0ctober 2020.
2. Clarke, M. (2017). 'The Belt and Road Initiative: China's New Grand Strategy?' *Asia Policy*, (24), pp. 71-79. Retrieved from https://www.jstor.org/stable/26403204, accessed on 22 September 2020.
3. Ministry of Commerce of the People's Republic of China. (2004, December 3). 'Vice-Minister of Commerce Ma Xiuhong made a Speech on "OECD" Global Forum on International Investment 2004'. Retrieved from http://maxiuhong2.mof com.gov.cn/article/speech/200412/20041200011104.shtml, accessed on 25 September 2020.
4. Kurlantzick, J. (2007). *Charm Offensive:How China's Soft Power is Transforming the World.* New Haven: Yale University Press. p. 88.
5. Yongmei, Y. (2004, January 7). 'UN report: China becoming major investor abroad.' (Z. Xiaoning, Interviewer). *People's Daily.* Retrieved from http://en.people.cn/200401/07/eng20040107_132003.shtml, accessed on 12 October 2020.
6. Belt and Road Forum for International Cooperation. (2017, April 10). 'Vision and Actions on Jointly Building Belt and Road.' Retrieved from http://beltandroad forum.org/english/n100/2017/0410/c22-45-4.html, accessed on 3 April 2020.
7. Ministry of Foreign Affairs of the People's Republic of China. (2015, March 28). 'Vision and Actions on Jointly Building Silk Road Economic Belt and 21st-Century Maritime Silk Road.' Retrieved from https://www.fmprc.gov.cn/mfa_eng/zxxx_662805/t1249618.shtml, accessed on 1 August 2020.
8. Saran, S. (2015, October 9). 'What China's One Belt and Road Strategy Means for India, Asia and the World.' *The Wire.* Retrieved from https://thewire.in/external-affairs/what-chinas-one-belt-and-one-road-strategy-means-for-india-asia-and-the-world, accessed on 15 July 2020.
9. Fang, X. (2015). 'The Belt and Road Initiative: Connecting China and Central Eurpe.' *International Issues and Slovac Foreign Policy Affairs*, 24(3), pp.3-14. Retrieved from https://www.jstor.org/stable/26591865?seq=11#metadata_info_tab_contents, accessed on 1 August 2020.
10. Shapiro, J. (2017, January 12). 'One Belt, One Road, No Dice.' *Geopolitical Futures.* Retrieved from https://geopoliticalfutures.com/one-belt-one-road-no-dice, accessed on 2 August 2020.
11. Ibid.
12. Hajari, N. (2018, November 2). 'Who Should be Afraid of One Belt One Road? China.' *The Print.* Retrieved from https://theprint.in/defence/who-should-be-afraid-of-one-belt-one-road-china/144136/, accessed on 3 August 2020.

13. Damuri, Y.R.; Perkasa, V.; Atje, R.; & Hirawan, F. (2019). *Perceptions and Readiness of Indonesia Towards The Belt and Road Initiative.* Indonesia: Centre for Strategic and International Studies. Retrieved from https://www.csis.or.id/uploads/attachments/post/2019/05/23/CSIS_BRI_Indonesia_r.pdf, accessed on 15 April 2020.
14. Yu, H. (2017). 'China's Belt and Road Initiative and its Implications for Southeast Asia.' *Asia Policy,* (24), pp. 117-122. Retrieved from https://www.jstor.org/stable/26403210, accessed on 4 August 2019.
15. Ibid.
16. Farr, G. (2017, July 10). 'Pakistan's Role In China's One Belt One Road Initiative'. *e-International Relations.* https://www.e-ir.info/2017/07/10/pakistans-role-in-chinas-one-belt-one-road-initiative/, accessed on 7 June 2021.
17. Putri, R. & Jeevan, J. (2018). 'The Implications of One Belt One Road (OBOR) Strategy on Malaysian Seaport Capacity.' *Advances in Transportation and logistics Reseach, 1,* pp. 652-667. Retrieved from https://proceedings.itltrisakti.ac.id/index.php/ATLR/article/view/70, accessed on 20 July 2020.
18. 'Malaysia Agrees to 14% Increase in East Coast Rail Link Project Costs.' (2021, April 6). *Railway Technology.* Retrieved from https://www.railway-technology.com/news/malaysia-east-coast-rail-link-project-costs/, accessed on 7 June 2021.
19. Hajari, op. cit.
20. Kuo, M. (2020, November 23). 'Malaysia in China's Belt and Road: Insights From Chow Bing Ngeow.' *The Diplomat.* Retrieved from https://thediplomat.com/2020/11/malaysia-in-chinas-belt-and-road/, accessed on 8 June 2021.
21. Parameswaran, P. (2019, April 23). 'Malaysia's Evolving Approach to China's Belt and Road Initiative.' *The Diplomat.* Retrieved from https://thediplomat.com/2019/04/malaysias-evolving-approach-to-chinas-belt-and-road-initiative/, accessed on 21 July 2020.
22. Kuo, op. cit.
23. Yhome, K. (2018, July 11). 'The BRI and Myanmar's China Debate'. Observer Research Foundation. Retrieved from https://www.orfonline.org/expert-speak/bri-myanmar-china-debate/, accessed on 8 June 2021.
24. 'Where Does Burma Stand on China's 'One Belt, One Road?'(2017, May 12). *The Irrawaddy.* Retrieved from: https://www.irrawaddy.com/opinion/editorial/burma-stand-chinas-one-belt-one-road.html, accessed on 21 August 2019.
25. Yhome, K., op. cit.
26. Chaudhury, D. R. (2021, July 26). 'Myanmar's Military Junta Revives Scope of BRI Projects.' *The Economic Times.* Retrieved from https://economictimes.indiatimes.com/news/international/world-news/myanmars-military-junta-revives-scope-of-bri-projects/articleshow/84739776.cms?from=mdr, accessed on 7 August 2021.
27. 'Myanmar Junta Implementing China's BRI Projects by Stealth. (2021, July 23). *The Irrawaddy.* Retrieved from https://www.irrawaddy.com/opinion/analysis/myanmar-junta-implementing-chinas-bri-projects-by-stealth.html, accessed on 7 August 2021.

28. Tower, J. & Clapp, P. A. (2021, June 8). 'Myanmar: China, the Coup and the Future.' United States Institute of Peace. Retrieved from https://www.usip.org/publications/2021/06/myanmar-china-coup-and-future, accessed on 20 July 2021.
29. Damuri, Y.; Perkasa, V.; Atje, R.; & Hirawan, F. op. cit., p. 9.
30. Laksmana, E. (2019, November 8). 'Indonesia as "Global Maritime Fulcrum": A Post-Mortem Analysis.' *Asia Maritime Transparency Initiative*. Retrieved from https://amti.csis.org/indonesia-as-global-maritime-fulcrum-a-post-mortem-analysis/, accessed on 15 October 2020.
31 Damuri, Perkasa, Atje, & Hirawan, op. cit., p. 21.
32. Ibid.
33. Parameswaran, P. (2019, July 9). 'Where is Indonesia on China's Belt and Road Initiative?' *The Diplomat*. Retrieved from https://thediplomat.com/2019/07/where-is-indonesia-on-chinas-belt-and-road-initiative/, accessed on 15 October 2020.
34. Palit, P. S. (2017). *Analysing China's Soft Power Strategy and Comparative Indian Initiatives*. New Delhi: Sage Publications India Pvt. Ltd., p. 48.
35. Grossman, D. (2020, June 11). 'What China Wants in South Asia.' Observer Research Foundation, (368), Retrieved from https://www.orfonline.org/research/what-china-wants-in-south-asia-67665/, accessed on 19 September 2020.
36. Jain, R. (2018). 'China's Economic Expansion in South Asia: Strengths, Challenges and Opportunities.' *International Journal of Asian Affairs*, 31 (1/2), pp. 21-36. Retrieved from https://www.jstor.org/stable/26608821, accessed on 20 August 2020.
37. M. S. Prathibha. (2017). 'China-Pakistan Economic Corridor.' In S. Kondapalli & H. Xiaowen (eds.), *One Belt One Road: China's Global Outreach*. New Delhi: Pentagon Press, p. 190.
38. Ibid.
39. Esteban, M. (2016). 'China-Pakistan Corridor: A Transit, Economic or Development Corridor.' *Strategic Studies*, 36 (2), pp. 63-74. Retrieved from https://www.jstor.org/stable/48535947, accessed on 25 July 2020.
40. Arshad, M. U. & Haidong, Z. (2017). 'China-Pakistan Economic Corridor (CPEC): Issues/Barrier and Imperatives of Pakistan and China.' *International Interdisciplinary Business-Economics Advancement Journal*, 2(2), pp. 104-114. Retrieved from DOI: 10.5038/2640-6489.2.2.1023, accessed on 21 August 2020.
41. Feng, D. (2021, April 19). 'BRI a Cornerstone for Growth in Pakistan.' *Global Times*. Retrieved from https://www.globaltimes.cn/page/202104/1221462.shtml, accessed on 30 June 2021.
42. Arshad. & Haidong, op. cit., p. 113.
43. Farr, op. cit.
44. 'CPEC Not Benefitting People of Balochistan: Provincial Minister'. (2021, February 6). *ANI*. Retrieved from https://www.aninews.in/news/world/asia/cpec-not-benefitting-people-of-balochistan-provincial-minister20210206160425/, accessed on 9 June 2021.
45. Farr, op. cit.

46. Chatterjee, A. (2020), 'Sri Lanka & the Belt and Road Initiative: A Balancing Act in the Indian Ocean Region.' *Defence and Security Journal*, 5, pp. 47-56. Retrieved from https://calhoun.nps.edu/bitstream/handle/10945/66470/Chatterjee-article%20%281%29.pdf?sequence=1&isAllowed=y, accessed on 15 July 2021.
47. Abi-Habib, M. (2018, June 25). 'How China Got Sri Lanka to Cough Up the Port.' *The New York Times*. Retrieved from https://www.nytimes.com/2018/06/25/world/asia/china-sri-lanka-port.html, accessed on 26 August 2020.
48. Press Trust of India. (2018, June 26). 'China's Acquisition of Sri Lankan Hambantota Port Highlights 'Debt Trap' to gain influence around World, Says Report.' *Firstpost*. Retrieved from https://www.firstpost.com/world/chinas-acquisition-of-sri-lankan-hambantota-port-highlights-debt-trap-to-gain-influence-around-world-says-report-4599911.html, accessed on 24 March 2021.
49. Samaranayake, N. (2021, March 2). 'Chinese Belt and Road Investment is not all Bad-or Good.' *Foreign Policy*. Retrieved from https://foreignpolicy.com/2021/03/02/sri-lanka-china-bri-investment-debt-trap/, accessed on 24 June 2021.
50. 'Perceptions of China's Belt and Road Initiative and Investments in Sri Lanka.' (2021, April 6). *Daily FT*. Retrieved from https://www.ft.lk/front-page/Perceptions-of-China-s-Belt-Road-Initiative-and-investments-in-Sri-Lanka/44-715870, accessed on 24 June 2021.
51. Hundlani, D. & Kannangara, P. (2020, May 7). 'The Belt and Road in Sri Lanka: Beyond the Debt Trap Discussion.' *The Diplomat*. Retrieved from https://thediplomat.com/2020/05/the-belt-and-road-in-sri-lanka-beyond-the-debt-trap-discussion/, accessed on 24 June 2021.
52. Saran, op. cit.
53. Macri, J. (2019, April 11). 'How Hungary's Path Leads to China's Belt and Roads.' *The Diplomat*. Retrieved from https://thediplomat.com/2019/04/how-hungarys-path-leads-to-chinas-belt-and-road/, accessed on 9 October 2020.
54. Than, K. & Komuves, A. (2020, April 24). Update 3—Hungary, China sign Loan Deal for Budapest-Belgrade Chinese Rail Project.' *Reuters*. Retrieved from https://www.reuters.com/article/hungary-china-railway-loan-idUSL5N2CC6A0, accessed on 9 October 2020.
55. *Eastern Opening*. (2018, May 21). 'The Orange Files.' Retrieved from https://theorangefiles.hu/eastern-opening/, accessed on 9 October 2020
56. Cabinet office of the Prime Minister. (2017, June 1). *Hungary is an Ideal Pillar of the One Belt, One Road*. Retrieved from https://miniszterelnok.hu/hungary-is-an-ideal-pillar-of-the-one-belt-one-road-initiative/ accessed on 10 October 2020.
57. Saran, op. cit.
58. Koutantou, A. (2021, May 28). *China's COSCO Hopes for Greek Deal on Piraeus Despite Delay-Official*. Reuters. Retrieved from https://www.reuters.com/article/us-cosco-ship-hold-greece-piraeus-idUSKCN2D91H7 accessed on 15 July 2021.
59. Bitabarova, A. (2018). 'Unpacking Sino-Central Asian Engagement along the New Silk Road: A Case Study of Kazakhstan.' *Journal of Contemporary East Asia*, 7 (2), pp. 149-173. Retrieved from https://www.tandfonline.com/doi/full/10.1080/

24761028.2018.1553226, accessed on 1 December 2020.

60. Ibid.
61. Yergaliyeva, A. (2019, October 24). 'Kazakh Government Estimates Nurly Zhol Program will cost $ 16.91 Billion Over Next Five Years.' *The Astana Times*. Retrieved from https://astanatimes.com/2019/10/kazakh-government-estimates-nurly-zhol-programme-will-cost-16-91-billion-over-next-five-years/, accessed on 1 December 2020.
62. Chazan, Y. (2020, January 24). 'China BRI Ventures Run into Trouble in Kazakhstan'. Asia Sentinel. Retrieved from https://www.asiasentinel.com/p/china-bri-ventures-run-into-trouble, accessed on 2 December 2020.
63. Standish, R. (2019, October 1). 'China's Path Forward is Getting Bumpy.' *The Atlantic*. Retrieved from https://www.theatlantic.com/international/archive/2019/10/china-belt-road-initiative-problems-kazakhstan/597853, accessed on 27 November 2020.
64. CGTN. (2019, June 14).'Tajikistan on 'Belt and Road' to further prosperity.' Retrieved from https://news.cgtn.com/news/2019-06-14/Tajikistan-on-Belt-and-Road-to-further-prosperity-HvKdOh1nfW/index.html, accessed on 27 November 2020.
65. Ibid.
66. Belt and Road Forum for International Cooperation. (2017, April 10). 'Vision and Actions on Jointly Building Belt and Road'. Retrieved from http://2017.beltandroadforum.org/english/n100/2017/0410/c22-45.html, accessed on 24 March 2021.

Chapter Five

Culture and Language as Instruments of Soft Power

Introduction

China is disseminating its culture and language in order to create a benign image. It is aptly using cultural diplomacy by promoting education, Confucius institutes, Chinese Diaspora, and tourism to promulgate China's culture and language. China's soft power is not just confined to institutional or individual levels. It is evident at the political level also. Former British Prime Minister David Cameron once stated that Britain should not stick to the traditional principles of offering German and French as foreign languages to students but should also emphasise on learning Mandarin.

Education

It has been observed that China is using education to spread Chinese culture and language with the help of two approaches. First, it is establishing Chinese educational institutions across the world and second, it is providing attractive programs and scholarships to students to study at Chinese universities. In 2017, the Chinese Ministry of Education issued a document indicating that the objective of their education reform initiative at the international level was to strengthen Chinese soft power so as to achieve its national interests. In order to enhance the capabilities of Chinese universities China has undertaken two initiatives, Project 985 and Project

211 aim at boosting about 100 higher education institutions and important disciplinary areas whereas Project 985 aims to establish world class universities. These attempts can possibly create opportunities for foreign students to study the Chinese language and culture.[1]

Alfred Marleku in his article titled '*Education as an Instrument of China's Soft Power*' has brought about similarities and also made a comparative analysis between UK and the USA on the one hand with China on other hand to examine the role of education in extending a country's influence. He has stated that generally, powerful countries start numerous scholarship programs to generate soft power. For instance, the Rhodes Scholarship Program of the United Kingdom spreads British imperialist values, the Fulbright Program of the USA spreads American values and the Patrice Lumumba University was established by the Soviet Union to instil values of Socialism. Likewise, China uses higher education to enhance its influence. China uses higher education to enhance its influence mainly in countries participating in BRI.

In some countries, education is treated as an industry while in others it has become a political tool. He has pointed out that developed countries welcome foreign students and charge them tuition fees which is more than the fees paid by domestic students. However, in China, foreign students enjoy generous financial support through scholarships and advanced study conditions, and accordingly, in 2018, the Chinese Foreign Ministry raised the budget by 16 per cent compared to 2017.[2]

The Chinese government has launched various programs to attract foreign students. On 13 March 2009, China's Ministry of Education (MOE) had published a circular on the Undergraduate Foundation Program for International Students in the Chinese Government Scholarship Program. It states that the MOE assigns responsibility to well-experienced higher education institutions (HEIs) in international education to commence the foundation program. The China Scholarship Council (CSC) will carry out admissions and management for the foundation program along with performing academic activities such as to frame the syllabus of compulsory courses and certain optional courses, to compile teaching materials and teaching reference books, and to slowly prepare a comprehensive evaluation system for assessment of the students' academic performance.[3]

The foundation program overtly promotes the Chinese language because it is mentioned in the circular that it is mandatory for all international students with Chinese government scholarships who undertake undergraduate programs taught in Chinese to enrol themselves for the foundation program. However, students who have not fulfilled such criteria are exempted from the foundation program provided they satisfy the following requirements. Those who submit proof issued by their secondary schools showing that Chinese is the instruction medium in the required courses of their secondary education and second those who hold copies of HSK certificate (generally valid for two years) that confirms their meeting the standards set for relevant disciplinary courses.[4]

The foundation program aims at introducing students to the basic knowledge of Chinese culture and society. It helps the students to understand the importance of acquiring communication skills in the Chinese language to handle daily life problems. The program also orients the students to learn basic Chinese vocabulary and grammar, and generally used expressions and patterns in Chinese for special purposes. Students can acquire basic competence in listening to Chinese, taking notes, and asking questions in class for disciplinary studies and basic reading skills with the help of dictionaries and reference books, and essential writing skills.

In 2014, President Xi Jinping, during his visit to South Asia, announced a Chinese initiative in the field of education to collaborate with South Asian countries.

He stated that 'China is emphasising on widening people-to-people and cultural exchanges with South Asia. It plans to offer 10,000 scholarships, training opportunities for 5,000 people, an exchange and training program for 5,000 youth and train 5,000 Chinese language teachers for South Asia in the next five years. In addition, China will work with South Asian countries to implement the China-South Asia Partnership Initiative for Science and Technology, give full play to the role of the

China-South Asia Expo, and build new platforms for mutually beneficial cooperation.[5]

A remarkable number of students from across the globe are taking education in China. In 2018 there were a total of 492,185 international students from 196 countries/areas pursuing their studies in 1,004 higher education institutions in China's 31 provinces/autonomous regions/ provincial-level municipalities, marking an increase of 3,013 students or 0.62 per cent compared to 2017.[6]

Number of international students by continent

Continent	*Number*
Asia	295,043
Africa	81,562
Europe	73,618
America	35,733
Oceania	6,229

Source: http://en.moe.gov.cn/documents/reports/201904/t20190418_378692.html

Number of international students by country of origin

Rank	*Country*	*Number*
No. 1	South Korea	50,600
No. 2	Thailand	28,608
No. 3	Pakistan	28,023
No. 4	India	23,198
No. 5	USA	20,996
No. 6	Russia	19,239
No. 7	Indonesia	15,050
No. 8	Laos	14,645
No. 9	Japan	14,230
No. 10	Kazakhstan	11,784
No. 11	Vietnam	11,299
No. 12	Bangladesh	10,735
No. 13	France	10,695
No. 14	Mongolia	10,158
No. 15	Malaysia	9,479

Source: http://en.moe.gov.cn/documents/reports/201904/t20190418_378692.html

Recently, China has concluded agreements with 54 countries on mutual recognition of qualifications and academic degrees in higher education. China has also built educational association and exchanges with 188 countries and regions and 46 international organisations. China has become the world's largest source of international students, as 1.4 million Chinese are currently studying abroad.[7]

Another notable drive carried out by the Chinese government is the Silk Road Belt and Road Initiative scholarship that covers Bachelor's, Master's and Ph.D. degrees in China. The popular Belt and Road Initiative, as established by the Chinese government, has a dedicated scholarship opened exclusively for international students. The prime criteria are that applicants must originate from countries located on the Belt and Road Project route.[8]

To attract a large number of foreign students, the Chinese government grants more than 10,000 scholarships for those students who wish to pursue studies in China through the Silk Road Scholarship Program. More than 60 per cent of the scholarships are assigned to countries impacted by the Belt Road.

P.K. Balachandran in his article titled '*China Vigorously Uses of Educational Facilities as Instruments of Soft Power*', has focused on the factor of financial affordability related to Chinese education. The high fees charged by profit-making Western universities are a deterrent to students from developing countries but Chinese universities, being mostly state-owned, do not lay stress on making money and are conveniently affordable. The average tuition fees in public universities in China range from US$ 3,300 to US$ 10,000 per year. Fees for an English-medium degree course are from US$ 2,200 to US$ 4,500 per year. On an average, foreign students spend around US$ 4,000 for accommodation and about US$ 2,000 for other living needs per year. It has been observed that American and British universities are costly. Tuition fees there start from US$ 8,000 and go up to US$ 15,000 a year. The total expenses of MBBS student per year in China is US$ 7,500 whereas in the UK it would be US$ 30,500 and in the USA, US$ 35,000. Even in India private colleges charge more that is US$ 14,700 a year.[9]

Confucius Institute (CI)

In China, being the highest populated country in the world, we found the maximum number of people speaking Mandarin as their first or second language while living in China. With the rise of China, however, growing numbers of people around the world are beginning to acquire Chinese as a second language. Since 2006, this process has been actively promoted by the Chinese government with the establishment of Confucius institutes in many different countries, often linked to local universities.[10]

Due to China's rapid economic growth and its assimilation in the world economy, there is an increase in demand for learning Chinese. China has witnessed the benefits received by the UK, France, Germany and Spain by promoting their national languages. Therefore, China has established Confucius institutes which are public institutes working on a non-profit basis. Their main objective is to promote the Chinese language and culture in foreign countries. The following table shows the approximate number of Confucius institutes and Confucius classrooms across the world.

Countries/Regions	*Confucius Institutes*	*Countries/Regions*	*Confucius Classrooms*
37 countries in Asia	137	24 countries in Asia	115
45 countries in Africa	62	20 countries in Africa	48
41 countries in Europe	187	31 countries in Europe	348
24 countries in North America	144	13 countries in North America	560
24 countries in South America	144	13 countries in South America	560

Source: https://www.cief.org.cn/qq#

'Hanban' is a public institution associated with the Chinese government. It promotes Chinese language and cultural teaching across the globe. Hanban used to finance and manage CIs before 2020. Since, 2020, the '*Chinese International Education Foundation*', an NGO, is working to spread Chinese language and culture by financing and managing CIs.[11]. The official site of the Chinese International Education Foundation has noted the aims and objectives of Confucius institutes which are comprehensive in nature. It states that the Confucius institutes are non-profit educational institutions, and jointly formed by China and foreign countries. They are dedicated to satisfy the needs of the people in learning Chinese, to impart knowledge of the Chinese language and culture, to deepen educational and cultural exchanges between China and other countries, to promote friendly relations between China and other countries, to boost multiculturalism and finally to establish a harmonious world.

Howard French has analyzed the usage of the name 'Confucius'. He noted that the name might seem odd in the context of China's increasing fondness for high-tech images. Nonetheless the carefully selected name indicates China's soft power aspirations. Using the name of the country's ancient and well-known philosopher for the institution bypasses any reference to official ideology of Marxism. In addition, Confucius represents harmony and peace; hence, the use of his name helps reduce fears about China's rapid rise.

Various articles on Confucius institutes discuss the experiences of teachers and students from China and other countries. It will be pertinent here to illustrate those experiences to understand the opinions about Confucius institutes. Jiang, who was awarded by the Chinese Education Ministry in 2008 for her contribution to Chinese teaching, highlighted the positive response by Bangladesh to the Chinese language. She mentioned that a good number of English-medium middle schools have made Chinese learning compulsory. A CI teacher from the University of Mumbai has observed that people from corporates, college students, and retired persons are interested in learning Mandarin. Ms. Xu lin, who took the responsibility to create the worldwide network of CIs, is of the opinion that there is a Chinese language craze in the world. With such responses it can be argued that 'mastering Chinese as a door to lucrative business opportunities, or simply as a matter of popular fashion, is suddenly in vogue'.[12]

The Chinese government has created an exam certification system (HSK), which determines the level of non-native speakers' knowledge of the Chinese language. Applicants must take the exam preparation course at the CI. After their level of language proficiency is determined, they have the opportunity to receive a grant to study in China. This current system and criteria push students to study the Chinese language and culture at a high level.[13]

Howard French has argued that different countries have accepted CIs by renouncing previous hostility with China. For example, due to Beijing's support for Communist rebels, Indonesia did ban the teaching of Chinese for three decades, but lifted it later. Vietnam has embraced Confucius institutes amidst a boom in Chinese language instruction despite sharing uneasy relations with China in the past. Apparently, Chinese has surpassed English as the most popular foreign language amongst students in South Korea, the country which fought beside America in a war against China.

In 2010, Ren Zhe in his article '*Confucius Institutes: China's Soft Power?*' has asserted that despite their rapid worldwide growth and popularity, CIs suffer from a host of international obstacles as well as from criticism within China. Furthermore, CIs play a limited role as extensions of China's soft power because they fail to account for contemporary aspects of Chinese culture. People question the purpose and ideology of CIs and believe their connection with the Chinese government acts as a hindrance to their expansion in top universities.[14]

Confucius institutes are facing challenges particularly in Western countries. Ananth Krishnan has recently penned an article in *The Hindu* titled, '*What are Confucius Institutes, and why are they under the scanner in India*'. He has very aptly explained the perceptions about the Confucius institutes around the world.

There is a debate in the West over arrangements of CIs. Some universities in Western countries were worried about the influence of the Chinese government on host institutions, which receive funding for running the CIs. Therefore, they have closed down CIs. Reports of such closures have come from the USA, Denmark, the Netherlands, Belgium, France and Sweden. In January, the CI in the University of Maryland, the first in the USA, closed down, citing new US rules, referring to the 2018 National Defence Authorisation Act, barring universities receiving from certain government assistance and accepting Chinese funding. Faced with this backlash, China is now rebranding the program. According to a recent directive from the Ministry of Education reported by the *South China Morning Post*, the Hanban has been renamed as the Centre for Language Education and Cooperation, with suggestions that the Confucius Institute brand may even be dropped.[15] However, these closures are minor in number. Confucius institutes and Confucius classrooms are still present in Africa, Central Asia, Latin America, and across Asia.

Growth of Confucius Institutes

Number of institutes in the world

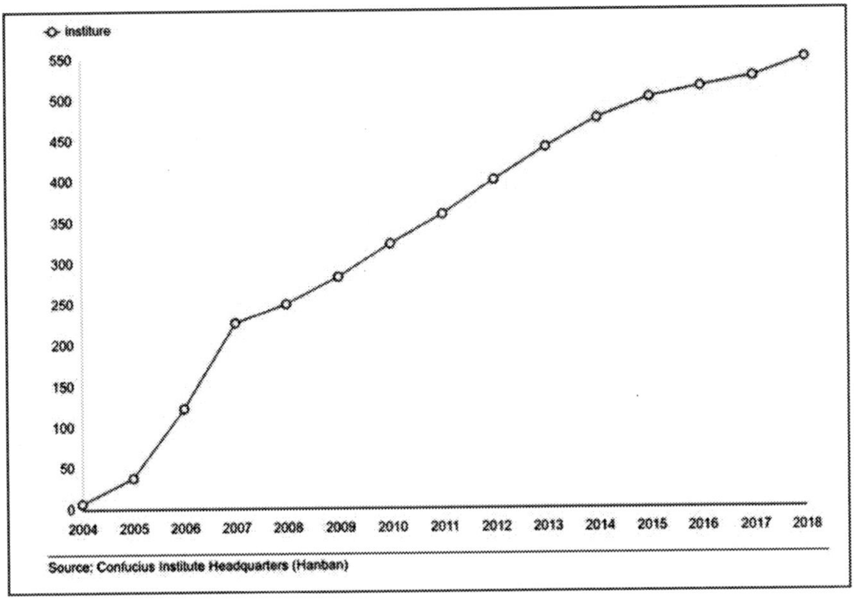

Source: https://www.bbc.com/news/amp/world-asia-china-49511231

According to critiques, CI is a way for Beijing to spread propaganda under the guise of teaching, interfere with free speech on campuses and even to spy on students.[16] They have further observed that CI branches present the situation in China subjectively. Ethnic and cultural diversity is promoted, but only in a manner approved by the Communist Party of China (CPC) and in such a way as to focus on the domination of the Hans.[17] CIs focus on conventional elements of Chinese culture like tea making or calligraphy. They are ready to avoid discussions on contentious issues. Important aspects of contemporary China such as the Uyghur minority, Tiananmen Square incident, Nobel Peace Prize for Chinese dissenter Liu Xiaobo are not discussed in CI programs. Links and topics which are put up on the CI's website generate a positive image of China.

Moreover, it has been observed that CI activities differ according to the regions in which they work. In African and Asian countries CI programs are linked to China's bilateral relations. CI achievements are highlighted, or new CI branches are opened during high-level visits. In America and European countries, CIs primarily focus on the popularisation of positive content about China and by spreading such information they try to prove that criticism of CIs are unjust. Despite the fact that language teaching has reportedly become a tool of foreign policy, the link between Confucius institutes and soft power is not, for many, readily evident. Debates have raged—and still do—over the ultimate aims of this project. Arguments for and against the institutes range from describing them as language institutes with no particular political connotation to presenting them as instruments of propaganda.[18]

It is interesting to note that an apparent lack of coordinated understanding even within the decision-making organs in China of what these institutes are, what 'culture' is, what aspects of it should be promoted abroad and what other sources of power become intertwined with cultural promotion. Clarifying these elements is a necessary analytical step for the evaluation of effectiveness, inasmuch as effectiveness is related to objectives and objectives are related to the way the initiative is conceived.[19] To assess the impact of CIs, one can discuss representative examples. This research seeks to examine the performance of CIs in Central Asia and Latin America.

Confucius Institutes in Central Asia

It would be apt to examine the role of CIs in Central Asia as the first pilot CI came into existence in Tashkent, Uzbekistan, before its official establishment in Seoul, South Korea. Nurlan Aliyev has very correctly described and analyzed the role of Confucius institutions in Central Asia. After 1991, elites and societies of the newly-established independent republics perceived China with fear or suspicion. These sentiments had their antecedents in Soviet propaganda promoting a negative image of China between the 1960s and 1980s. Limited knowledge of Chinese culture and society, language and religious differences also influenced the public mood. Moreover, China's increasing economic involvement in the region and especially the increasing number of Chinese farmers renting land in Central Asia amplified these perceptions.[20]

It was expected that CIs and Confucius classrooms would be effective instruments to change the perception about China in Central Asia. China wanted to create its charm by eliminating hostility, biases and threat perceptions which were developed during the Soviet era. At present, there are a total of 13 CIs in Central Asia.

Countries	*Confucius Institutes*
Kazakhstan	05
Kyrgyzstan	04
Tajikistan	02
Uzbekistan	02

Source: https://www.cacianalyst.org/publications/analytical-articles/item/13599-chinas-soft-power-in-central-asia.html

The increase in the number of CIs since 2004 implies an upsurge in the number of students studying in them. For example, 22,270 students of Central Asia were at CIs immediately after their inception. Hence, scholars assert that eventually the number of young people welcoming Chinese culture would increase. China employs CIs 'to strengthen its cultural influence in Central Asia, using the geographical coverage method. For example, CIs in Kazakhstan are located in the east and west, in the south and north, like chess pieces. In Uzbekistan and Kyrgyzstan and Tajikistan they are positioned in large cities.[21]

According to experts, China has yet to develop a strong concept of cultural diplomacy but promoting the Chinese language has resulted in visible results in recent years. Central Asian youth prefer learning Chinese. They look to China as a source of careers and income.

Aliyev, N. in his article has mentioned that despite the increase of Chinese soft power influences in Central Asia in recent years, they remain limited for now, especially when compared to the influence exercised by Russia and the West. However, the role of the Russian language and culture is decreasing in the region, and a significant share of the young well-educated class, which will form the future political elites, has studied either in the West or China. China is likely to increase its cultural and educational involvement in the region in coming years and has built friendly relations with local political elites. However, for Central Asian states, the possibility of balancing between east, north and west remains a precondition for avoiding becoming clients to any one power.[22]

Confucius Institutes in Latin America

China's economic cooperation with Latin American Countries (LAC) is at its peak. China has acquired the status of a top trading partner for countries like Brazil, Chile, Peru and Uruguay.[23] Despite the lack of historical links and geographical remoteness, its cultural diplomacy in the region is slowly taking shape and its credit goes to the CIs. So far, China has established 31 CIs in LACs.

Ricardo Martinez, staff associate and legislative aide at the US House of Representatives has interactions with students of CI in PUC-Rio, Brazil. Students there said that the CI has become a cultural and educational bridge between China and Brazil. It is good start if someone wants to learn about China. Ricardo Martinez found that discussions on China have not remained confined to public policy.[24] Even Brazilian students curiously talk about China's economic growth. Samantha Gray, 43–year-old business woman, who is learning Chinese from CI in Venezuela believes that Chinese is more important than English. Randy Moreno, 30 years old, from Falcon state said that learning Chinese would be helpful in his career. He would like to become a translator for a Chinese company.[25]

Patricio Giusto, a public policy expert and academician, is optimistic about the performance of Confucius institutes in Latin America. During an interview in *Xinhua* he said "Confucius Institutes in Latin America are increasing awareness of Chinese culture and promoting China's vision of setting up a community with a shared future for mankind." He has completed his post-graduation in Chinese studies from Zhejiang University in China. He claimed that the Confucius institutes are crucial. They are tools of Chinese cultural promulgation abroad. He pointed out that young people are interested in learning Chinese. He further suggested that China should tap such an opportunity and should take efforts to satisfy their interests.[26]

Norberto Consani, founder of the National University of La Plata (UNLP's) Centre for Chinese Studies and the current Argentine director of its Confucius Institute stated that China's influence in Latin America is different than American influence. China had suffered humiliation from the Western powers. So, it prefers equality which has led to the horizontal relationship between China and LACs. On the contrary, the USA comes with a zero-sum policy.[27]

Lucia He has rightly explained the cordial relations between Argentinean and Chinese students. During the school year, the corridors of the institute at UNLP are crowded with Argentinean students and Chinese foreign exchange students, as well as teachers from both countries. The atmosphere is one of total convergence between Argentinean and Chinese cultures, where *yerba mate* sits side by side with green tea leaves on classroom shelves and students greet each other with a friendly 'hola' followed by a 'ni hao'.[28]

Li Fangjun, English professor at Xi'an International Studies University and Consani's Chinese counterpart at UNLP, is of the opinion that, CIs in Latin America contribute to the advancement of China's economic interests. In Belt and Road Initiative (BRI) projects local enterprisers in LACs will come into contact with Chinese enterprisers. Hence, for the smooth implementation of BRI, locals need to communicate in Chinese and need to have better understanding of China. He further added that Confucius institutes are complementary to BRI. Araujo, young expert in calligraphy, is convinced of the inevitability of China and the Chinese language. He said that people who understand Chinese and China will have an upper hand in the future.[29]

Chinese Diaspora

The concept of a Chinese Diaspora can be understood with the help of two Chinese terms, '*huaqiao* and *huaren*'.[30] 'Huaqiao' means Chinese citizens living overseas and 'huaren' implies ethnic Chinese but now have become foreign citizens. The Chinese government has been trying to treat these communities differently. Hence, Huaqiao is incorporated under domestic affairs and huaren is included under foreign affairs. Nonetheless, according to observers, the difference between the two is getting blurred day by day, particularly under Xi Jinping. Currently, every Chinese person is considered to serve the projects and dreams of the 'motherland' by their virtue of being ethnic Chinese. As it has been observed, it is also expected from overseas students.

Historically, the Chinese Diaspora in Southeast Asia was the most important, although the Chinese of Hong Kong, Macau, and Taiwan were similarly elevated to a priority after the 1950s. During the 1980s, following the new wave of outward migration, there was also renewed attention to the Chinese Diaspora in North America.[31] Chinese external migration is becoming more geographically diversified, and Chinese communities are emerging in Africa, Latin America, Europe and Oceania.

Martin Jacquesin in his article, '*As China's power grows, the Diaspora starts to flex its worldwide muscle*' has pointed out the features of the Chinese Diaspora. First, it is numerically large and spread all over the globe, from Africa to Europe, east Asia to the Americas. Second, for historical and cultural reasons, it enjoys an unusually strong identification with the Middle Kingdom. Third, China is already a global power and destined to become perhaps the most powerful country in the world. And as its rise continues, as Chinese worldwide interests grow exponentially, the Chinese Diaspora is likely to expand greatly; become increasingly prosperous, be buoyed by China's own economic success; enjoy growing prestige as a result of China's rising status; and feel an even closer affinity with China.[32]

Sheng Dingan, associate professor at Bloomsburg University, opines that '*Since the end of cold war, China's national image has been constantly haunted by its human rights records and the China threat theory. Against this backdrop, overseas Chinese have become a valuable platform for China's national image management*'.[33] The Chinese Diaspora had supported China in the anti-China protests ahead on the 2008 Beijing Olympics. Martin Jacques has mentioned that though in London, Paris, Athens and San

Francisco pro-Tibet demonstrators were more than the supporters of the Olympic Games, the Chinese Diaspora effectively protected Chinese interests abroad. More than 10,000 Chinese Australians staged the biggest pro-Beijing rally in Canberra.[34] In Seoul, thousands turned out in support, as they did in Nagano in Japan, in both cases dwarfing the number of protesters; likewise in Kuala Lumpur, Jakarta, Bangkok, Ho Chi Minh City and Hong Kong.[35]

However, it is claimed that the Chinese authorities orchestrated pro-Beijing demonstrations, deployed their own security, and made behind-the-scenes threats to activists, all while denying such measures—a strategy repeated across four continents along the torch relay.[36] Contrary to these findings, Martin Jacques has advocated the Chinese Diaspora's contribution and argued that our "view of these events is shaped by our Western mindset. The problem is that as the global centre of gravity tilts away from the West, it is becoming increasingly important to look beyond our assumptions and gain a wider picture".[37]

The Chinese Diaspora has exported Chinese culture to different parts of the world. In fact, overseas Chinese are responsible for social, political and cultural consequences in host countries. In the process of migration, the ethnic Chinese have passed on goods like Chinese medicines, food and science. They represent oriental culture. Therefore, Westerners find it appealing and interesting. Chinese festivals are becoming popular; for instance, Chinese Lunar New Year celebrations are hosted by London's Trafalgar Square. The Chinese Diaspora has cultivated ethnic ties. For example, the Indonesian government has legalised the right of the ethnic Chinese to become naturalised citizens.[38] Jakarta has also launched the policy of cultural pluralism and has provided religious liberties. It has incorporated the Chinese language into the secondary school syllabus and invited teachers from China.

Although China has no official religion, and declares itself to be a Communist state, Beijing is promoting the country as a Buddhism hub. Buddhism is popular with homeland Chinese and hence, the Chinese Diaspora in Southeast Asia have always portrayed a Buddhist-friendly ima towards the locals of the region. This has encouraged more bil engagements in the region organised by Buddhist institutions. Vesak, a Buddhist festival (marking birth, enlightenment and death of Buddha), has its significance in ASEAN nations.[39] Since 2012, Southeast Asian countries host China-ASEAN music festivals. It has strengthened the link with ethnic Chinese in the region. There is an increase in the number of ASEAN's Chinese media houses like newspapers, magazines, TV channels, radio stations and Chinese websites. They promote the Chinese language and culture.

Overseas Chinese students fit into both the roles as the Chinese Diaspora and as a part of China's policy of the internationalisation of education. As overseas Chinese, they promote the Chinese language and culture in host countries and as a part of the policy of the internationalisation of education they represent narratives formulated by the Chinese government.

The Chinese Diaspora has created challenges for themselves as well as for locals. For instance, in Johannesburg, South Africa, cultural tensions are often felt between the black and Chinese communities, especially since Chinese business is often in direct competition with black business, which is heavily supported by the government's Black Economic Empowerment Policy (BEE).[40]

Tourism

China has become the official language of the United Nations World Tourism Organisation in January 2021. It indicates the popularity of the Chinese language worldwide. It could be argued that tourism has played a key role in enhancing the weightage of the Chinese language. With the development of China's domestic and foreign tourism, tourism practitioners in many countries have long realised the importance of mastering Chinese, and the demand for learning Chinese is increasing day by day. To this end, Chinese teaching institutions in various countries have opened various "Chinese + Tourism" special courses and training to meet people's growing learning needs.[41]

As the Middle Kingdom moves to expand its influence, President Xi Jinping is steering China to the top of the global powers list with an emphasis on the key signals of an empire: controlling territory well beyond one's borders either through soft or hard (military) power.[42] China as the world's second largest economy has extended its power by being the most influential buyer of goods and supplier of everything from cars to electronics. It has now discovered a new weapon: the millions of Chinese who travel overseas.

The China National Tourism Administration was looking after the affairs of tourism, but it was replaced by the Ministry of Culture and Tourism of the People's Republic of China established in 2018. It promotes tourism in China. Besides, there is a 'China Tourism Academy'[43] (CTA) which was set up in 2008.

The CTA aims at establishing itself as a institute for government, brainpower of the industry and experts specialised in boosting the development and international exchange of China's tourism industry, with emphasising on research on basic theories, policies as well as crucial but difficult issues related to the development of tourism, studying, collating and verifying tourism development plans, providing technical support to the scrutiny of tourism development plans proposed by local governments, organising high-level training and professional talents in the tourism sector and managing international and domestic academic exchanges.

China has come up with an interesting and detailed report on tourism in China. It starts with the assertion that, traditionally, in international relations, power is understood in the context of either threats or coercion. Countries are interested in enhancing their image and interests by persuading others to support them. China uses this strategy for enhancing its soft power by various means such as language, culture, trade, and tourism.

As a source of revenue and a means of enhancing its international image, tourism is becoming essential for China. In 2018, nearly 159 million 'visitors' travelled to China. This figure includes all non-residents travelling to China for any length of time or purpose. That same year, China received

62.9 million 'tourists'—travellers staying in the country for at least one night.[44]

Tourism renders tremendous economic benefits to China. In 2018, China ranked second in world travel and tourism for this sector's contribution to GDP ($ 1.5 trillion) and first in the world among top earners for its contribution to employment (79.9 million jobs). That same year, China invested $ 155 bn in its tourism infrastructure, a figure second only to that of the USA ($ 176.3 bn). Overall, tourism and travel accounted for 11 per cent of China's total GDP in 2018.[45] It is estimated by the World Travel and Tourism Council that the contribution of travel and tourism of China to its economy will be more by 2028.[46]

The report also highlights the use of tourism by the Chinese government to create a benign image. The Chinese government has got an opportunity to indirectly shape international politics due to China's increasing share in international tourism and the financial impact of Chinese tourists. The Chinese government tends to use tourism as a measure to improve the world view of China. At the same time, it threatens to limit Chinese tourists' visits to certain countries.

The Chinese language and tourism act complementarily and create a benign image of China. As people are excited about learning Chinese, educational institutions in various countries have launched various 'Chinese + Tourism' courses and training. In 2017, Indonesia's Udayana University and Hasanuddin University co-established Indonesia's first Tourism Chinese Training Centre. The centre cooperates with the tourism department of Bali. International Chinese teachers sent by the Language Cooperation Centre provide practical Chinese tourism intensive courses and on-the-job training courses for travel agencies, hotels, tourism service departments and management departments that receive Chinese tourists. They carry out exchanges of experts to give lectures, exchanges of teachers, exchanges of students for internships, etc., and strengthen cooperation with Chinese tourism colleges.[47]

Public Chinese training courses are popular amongst local students in Phuket. The training content includes 'greeting', 'numbers', 'pick-up', 'check-in' and 'check-out', from shallow to deep, step by step, and diversified practice methods which can comprehensively improve students' listening, speaking, reading and writing skills.[48]

A large number of Chinese tourists come to Pokhara, Nepal, every year. Under the BRI, the National Tourism Administration of Nepal hosts a 'Nepal-Pokhara Tourism Chinese Training Course'. International Chinese teacher volunteers from China are teaching Chinese courses to 70 students in Pokhara. These students are staff from the local tourism bureau, hotel managers, and shop owners. They will complete 80 hours of Chinese courses in two months.[49]

Conclusion

Nye's emphasis on culture as the core of soft power finds increasing resonance in China's conduct of external engagement.[50] It includes different initiatives, and activities for the purpose of advancing national interests.[51] It has been observed that culture has been inseparable from politics in China, highlighting the salience of the context and a prominent role by state actors.[52] Cultural diplomacy (CD) is very natural. While charting ambitious goals of economic and social developments for the 1.3 bn people in the next five years and by 2020, Hu Jintao also stressed the need to enhance Chinese culture as the country's 'soft power' in his keynote speech to the 17th National Congress of the Communist Party of China (CPC).[53] It could be concluded that China's success of cultural diplomacy with education, Confucius institutes, Chinese Diaspora and tourism differs from place to place. As China offers scholarships, students are optimistic about pursuing education from China. Though, in the West, there is pessimism about the Confucius institutes, in Latin America and Central Asia, Confucius institutes are creating a benign image of China. It will be too early to judge the success of the Chinese Diaspora and tourism as a tool of cultural diplomacy.

NOTES

1. China Education Centre. (n.d). 'Complete Guide to China Scholarships: Two Approaches to Study in China on Scholarship'. Retrieved from https://www.chinaeducenter.com/en/cedu/ceduproject211.php, accessed on 15 November 2020.
2. Marleku, A. (2019, April 9). 'Education as an Instrument of China's Soft Power'. TRT World. Retrieved https://www.trtworld.com/opinion/education-as-an-instrument-for-china-s-soft-power-25699, accessed on 19 November 2020.
3. Ministry of Education, People's Republic of China. (2009, March 13). 'Circular of the Ministry of Education on Undergraduate Foundation Program for International Students on the Chinese Government Scholarship Program'. Retrieved from http://en.moe.gov.cn/documents/laws_policies/201506/t20150626_191403.html, accessed on 20 November 2020.
4. Ibid.
5. Liu, S. (2014, October 16). '*"China Threat" in South Asia: A Perspective from China*'. Institute of Peace and Conflict Studies. Retrieved from http://www.ipcs.org/comm_select.php?articleNo=4695, accessed on 30 November 2020.
6. Ministry of Education, The People's Republic of China. (2019, April 18). 'Statistical Report on International Students in China for 2018. Retrieved from http://en.moe.gov.cn/documents/reports/201904/t20190418_378692.html, accessed on 20 November 2020.
7. 'China Forges Agreement with 54 Countries on Mutual Recognition of Higher Education Degrees.' (2020, September 5). *Xinhua Net.* Retrieved from http://www.xinhuanet.com/english/2020-09/05/c_139345581.htm, accessed on 22 November 2020.
8. *China Scholar.* (n.d.). 'China Belt and Road Scholarship.' Retrieved from https://www.china-scholar.com/scholarships/belt-and-road-initiative-scholarships-bri/. accessed on 15 October 2020.
9. Balchandran, P. K. (2018, May 24). 'China Vigorously Uses Educational Facilities as Instruments of Soft Power.' *The Citizen.* Retrieved from https://www.thecitizen.in/index.php/en/NewsDetail/index/5/13865/Chinas-VigorOf-Educational-Facilities-As-Instruments-Of-Soft-Power, accessed on 22 October 2020.
10. Jacques, M. (2009). *When China Rules the World.* New York: The Penguin Press. p. 399.
11. Xi, C. (2020, July 5). 'New NGO to Operate China's Confucius Institutes, 'disperse misinterpretation'. *Global Times.* Retrieved from https://www.globaltimes.cn/content/1193584.shtml, accessed on 10 November 2020.
12. French, H. W. (2006, April 1). Another Chinese Export Is All the Rage: China's Language.' *The New York Times.* Retrieved from https://www.nytimes.com/2006/01/11/world/asia/another-chinese-export-is-all-the-rage-chinas-language.html, accessed on 2 November 2020.
13. Kwrimbaev, E.; Mukhametkhanuly, N.; Turgenbay, A. & Nabizhankyzy, Z. (n.d.).

Main Factors of China's Soft Power in Central Asia. CA & C Press AB Publishing House. Retrieved from https://www.ca-c.org/online/2020/journal_eng/cac-01/02.shtml#_ednref9, accessed on 2 June 2021.

14. Zhe, R. (2010, June 22). 'Confucius Institutes: China's Soft Power?' *Rising Powers Initiative*. Retrieved from https://www.risingpowersinitiative.org/2010/06/22/confucius-institutes-chinas-soft-power/, accessed on 2 November 2020.
15. Krishnan, A. (2020, August 9). 'What are Confucius Institutes, and why are they under the scanner in India.' *The Hindu*. Retrieved from https://www.thehindu.com/news/national/the-hindu-explains-what-are-confucius-institutes-and-why-are-they-under-the-scanner-in-india/article32306693.ece, accessed on 15 November 2020.
16. Jakhar, P. (2019, September 6). 'Confucius Institutes: The Growth of China's Controversial Cultural Branch.' *BBC News*. Retrieved from https://www.bbc.com/news/amp/world-asia-china-49511231, accessed on 22 October 2020.
17. Przychodniak, M. (2019, May 8). 'Confucius Institutes: A Tool For Promoting China's Interests.' CHOICE. Retrieved from https://chinaobservers.eu/confucius-institutes-as-a-tool-for-promoting-chinas-interests/, accessed on 20 October 2020.
18. Procopio, M. (2015, July). 'The Effectiveness of Conficius Institutes as a Tool of China's Soft Power in South Africa.' *African East-Asian Affairs*, (2), pp. 98-125. Retrieved from https://www.researchgate.net/publication/282840886_The_effectiveness_of_Confucius_Institutes_as_a_tool_of_China's_soft_power_in _South _ Africa, accessed on 23 October 2020.
19. Ibid.
20. Aliyev, N. (2019, December 19). 'China's Soft Power in Central Asia.' *The Central Asia Caucasus ANALYST*. Retrieved fromhttps://www.cacianalyst.org/publications/analytical-articles/item/13599-chinas-soft-power-in-central-asia.html, accessed on 23 October 2020.
21. Kwrimbaev, Mukhametkhanuly, Turgenbay, Nabizhankyzy, op. cit.
22. Aliyev, op. cit.
23. Yu, R. (2020, March 29). 'China's Public Diplomacy Strategy in Latin America and Caribbean.' *Sigma Iota Rho Journal of International Relations*. Retrieved from http://www.sirjournal.org/op-ed/2020/3/29/chinas-public-diplomacy-strategy-in-latin-america-and-the-caribbean, accessed on 3 November 2020.
24. Martinez, R. (2018, July 6). 'China's Confucius Institutes in Brazil –An Educational Exchange Powerhouse?' *Linkedin*. Retrieved from https://www.linkedin.com/pulse/chinas-confucius-institutes-brazil-educational-ricardo-martinez, accessed on 2 November 2020.
25 Gibbs, S. (2019, October 15). *Mandarin Classes in Venezuela on the Rise.* CGTN America. Retrieved from https://america.cgtn.com/2019/10/13/mandarin-classes-in-venezuela-on-the-rise, accessed on 5 November 2020.
26. Aires, B. (2018, May 7). 'Interview: Confucius Institutes Bridge LatAm, Chinese Cultures.' *Xinhua Net*. Retrieved from http://www.xinhuanet.com/english/2018-05/07/c_137161363.htm, accessed on 5 November 2020.
27. He, L. W. (2019, April 12). 'How China is Closing the Soft Power Gap in Latin

America.' *Americas Quarterly*. Retrieved from https://www.americasquarterly.org/article/how-china-is-closing-the-soft-power-gap-in-latin-america/, accessed on 24 October 2020.

28. Ibid.
29. Ibid.
30. Wai, C. S. (2017, April 30). 'China's 'One Big Family Policy Raises Concerns.' *The Straits Times*. Retrieved from https://www.straitstimes.com/opinion/chinas-one-big-family-policy-raises-concerns, accessed on 10 November 2020.
31. An, W. X. (2019). 'China's Evolving Policy towards the Chinese Diaspora in Southeast Asia (1949-2018*)*.' ISEAS Yusof Ishak Institute (14), pp. 1-25. Retrieved from https://eresources.nlb.gov.sg/printheritage/detail/2ed87b51-1fe2-44b0-876b-1a46fc4accea.aspx, accessed on 22 October 2020.
32. Jacques, M. (2008, June 11). As China's Power Grows the Diaspora Starts to Flex its Worlwide Muscle.' *The Guardian*. Retrieved from https://www.theguardian.com/commentisfree/2008/jun/11/china.comment, accessed on 23 October 2020.
33. Ding, S. (2014, April). 'Chinese Soft Power and Public Diplomacy: An Analysis of China's New Diaspora Engagement policies in Xi Era.' *East Asia Institute*. Retrieved from http://www.eai.or.kr/data/bbs/eng_report/201404011627122.pdf, accessed on 22 October 2020.
34. 'Timeline: Olympic Torch Protests around the World'. (2008, April 28). *Reuters*. Retrieved from https://www.reuters.com/article/us-olympics-torch-disruptions-idUSSP17070920080428, accessed on 23 October 2020.
35. Jacques 2008, op, cit.
36. Ebrahimian, B. A. and Dorfman, Z. (2019, May 14). 'China has been Running Global Influence Campaigns for Years, '*The Atlantic*. https://www.theatlantic.com/international/archive/2019/05/beijing-olympics-china-influence-campaigns/589186/ , accessed on 20 November 2020.
37. Jacques, 2008, op, cit.
38. Larin, A. (2014, January 16). 'The Chinese Diaspora in Southeast Asia: Gains and Losses.' Russian International Affairs Council. Retrieved from https://russiancouncil.ru/en/analytics-and-comments/analytics/the-chinese-diaspora-in-southeast-asia-gains-and-losses/, accessed on 23 October 2020.
39. Sooriyan, A. (2018, August 27). 'The Unofficial Ambassadors: A Comparative Study of Indian and Chinese Diaspora in Southeast Asia.' Chennai Centre for China Studies. Retrieved from https://www.c3sindia.org/culture-history/the-unofficial-ambassadors-a-comparative-study-of-indian-and-chinese-diaspora-in-southeast-asia-by-anusha-sooriyan/, accessed on 23 October 2020.
40. Academy for Cultural Diplomacy. (n.d.). 'Chinese Diaspora'. Retrieved from https://www.culturaldiplomacy.org/academy/index.php?chinese-diaspora, accessed on 24 October 2020.
41. Centre For Language Education And Cooperation. (2021, February 2*)*. 'China Becomes the Official Language of United Nations World Tourism Organization, and the Development of "Chinese+Goes" Further.' Retrieved from http://

www.chinese.cn/page/#/pcpage/article?id=499, accessed on 28 February 2021.

42. Tan, H. (2016, August 11). 'President Xi Expands China's Soft Power Through Tourism'. *CNBC.* Retrieved from https://www.cnbc.com/2016/08/10/president-xi-expands-chinas-soft-power-through-tourism.html, accessed on 16 November 2020.
43. China Tourism Academy (Data Centre for Ministry of Culture and Tourism). Retrieved from http://eng.ctaweb.org.cn/, accessed on 18 November 2020.
44. *China Power.* (n.d.). 'Is China Attracting Foreign Visitors'. Retrieved from https://chinapower.csis.org/tourism/, accessed on 16 November 2020.
45. Ibid.
46. Ibid.
47. Centre For Language Education And Cooperation, op. cit.
48. Ibid.
49. Ibid.
50. Palit, P. S. (2017). *Analysing China's Soft Power Strategy and Comparative Indian Initiatives.* New Delhi: Sage Publications Inida Pvt. Ltd., p. 11.
51. Kang, H. (n.d.). 'Reframing Cultural Diplomacy: International Cultural Politics of Soft Power and the Creative Economy.' Retrieved from https://www.culturaldiplomacy.org/academy/content/pdf/participant-papers/2011-08-loam/Reframing-Cultural-Diplomacy-International-Cultural-Politics-of-Soft-Power-and-the-Creative-Economy-Hyungseok-Kang.pdf, accessed on 25 October 2020.
52. Palit, op. cit., p. 12.
53. 'Hu Urges Enhancing Soft Power of Chinese Culture.' (2007, October 15). *China Daily*. Retrieved from https://www.chinadaily.com.cn/china/2007-10/15/content_6226620.htm, accessed on 5 November 2020.

Chapter Six
Conclusion

Post-Cold War international relations had undergone several changes. Globalisation and interdependence had become keys of international relations. America proved itself as the strongest economic and military power against the backdrop of a multi-polar world order. Traditional and non-traditional factors were equally shaping global politics. One remarkable phenomenon of that period was rising China. Thirty years ago, no one could have imagined China's emergence as the second largest economy in the world and the status of Mandarin as the most widely spoken language in the world.

In 1978, China introduced economic reforms and concentrated on domestic economic growth. Since the 1990s, it has been pro-active at the international level. Deng Xiaoping's 'Reform and Open Door', Jiang Zemin's 'Three Represents', Hu Jintao's 'Peaceful Development' and Xi Jinping's 'Chinese Dreams' have guided China's domestic and foreign policy. The notion of soft power was introduced in China's foreign policy in the late 1990s. Slowly, it began to employ economic and cultural tools to shape world politics.

It is evident that as a practice, soft power is an old phenomenon. For example, in order to restore its reputation after the defeat in the Franco-Prussian war, France established the Alliance Francaise in 1883 to promote French culture and language. Currently there are 832 institutes of Alliance Francaise in 131 countries.[1] The Goethe Institute was formed in 1951 to spread German culture and language. At present, there are 157 Goethe institutes in 98 countries.[2] However, Joseph Nye is the first person who has systematically elaborated the term. He has argued that in a multi-polar world no country can depend upon mere hard power. It should utilise culture, policy and values to achieve its national interests. He defined soft power as the ability to attract people without coercion. He also named the tools of soft power—culture, political values and foreign policy. Though China is a newcomer in the field of soft power, it has been observed that it is employing the instruments of soft power such as trade, investment and culture and language to exert its influence.

Yong Deng in an edited book titled '*Soft Power: China's Emerging Strategy in International Politics*' has evaluated the reasons for the dearth of explicit interest in soft power in China. He stated that first, Chinese experts had attributed the concept of soft power to the West or the USA because they believed that the discourse in international relations was dominated by the West. Hence, Chinese analysts thought that China should protect itself against such subtle forms of power. Second, China had witnessed the catastrophic foreign relations in the 1990s. For example, instability in China-America relations due to the human rights issues in China, Taiwan crisis and unintended bombing of the Chinese embassy in Belgrade.[3]

Meanwhile, the China threat theory had occupied Western debates which portrayed China as an aggressive and harmful actor. At the same time, America displayed its presence in the West Pacific to ensure its security commitment towards the region. Against this background, Chinese leaders realised the need to promote a positive image of China. Moreover, events between 1997 and 1998 boosted China's quest of co-operative, economic and multilateral diplomacy. The nuclear proliferation crisis in South Asia led to collaboration between the USA and China. The Asian financial crisis contributed to the transformation in China-ASEAN relations. Gradually, the topic of soft power and its possible tools received attention in China. In the early days, Chinese experts highlighted culture as an instrument of soft power. Later, they began to consider other tools like the Beijing consensus as various developing and underdeveloped countries were astonished by the Chinese model of economic development.[4]

Subsequently, to diminish the fears about the 'China Threat', the Chinese government came up with the term 'Peaceful Development'. The official document on 'China's Peaceful Development' indirectly attempts to create China's image as a responsible country and thus spreading its benign image across the globe. The document highlights China's responsibility to contribute to world peace via its own development and to promote mutual benefit.[5] China's leaders noted the relevance of soft power. Hu Jintao explicitly mentioned soft power by underlining the significance of Chinese culture at the 17th National Congress of the Chinese Communist Party. He stressed to popularise Chinese culture and facilitate international cultural exchanges through which the influence of Chinese culture could be enhanced. In 2014, Xi Jinping encouraged the augmentation of China's soft power and to provide a good Chinese narrative.

With the help of the study of China's foreign policy in general and its soft power in particular, this book attempts to examine the hypothesis that China has developed its own notion of soft power. It is using soft power instruments to create convergence of its own national interests with that of others. It can be stated that China traces the roots of its soft power notion back to Chinese philosophy. For example, the Chinese philosophy of self-cultivation implies that a cultivated person can legitimately lead the world. To achieve domestic growth (self-cultivation) China requires a peaceful environment. Through the Belt and Road Initiative (BRI), China is facilitating its domestic growth as well as developing participants which might eventually allow it to legitimately lead the world. The principle of 'mandate of heaven' focuses on good words and good deeds to acquire the consent of the ruler. It is evident in China's 'Go Global' strategy and free trade agreements through which Chinese ambassadors and ministers have used good words and deeds plus time and again underlined the concept of mutual benefits to portray a benign image. Hence, it is discernible that China's soft power tools—trade, investment, culture and language—reflect its pursuit to create convergence of interests, thereby commanding legitimacy.

Trade has occupied a significant position in China's external relations since it has unleashed its economic capabilities. It seems that China's free trade agreements have produced results in favour of China. Free trade agreements of Western countries are comprehensive in nature. In the case of China, they are limited and provide scope for further development. It has led to the growing dependence of other countries on China. In some cases, China offers concessions like the early harvest program which develops a positive image of China. Despite generating FTAs, countries face a deficit in trade with China. Yet, they upgrade FTAs with China like ASEAN, Pakistan, etc. Trade with China gives them access to lucrative Chinese markets.

BRI is considered a milestone in China's investment policy. China has carried out huge infrastructure projects in different parts of the world Like, for instance, Malaysia's East Coast Rail Link, Indonesia's Jakarta Bandung High Speed Rail Projects, Pakistan's China-Pakistan Economic Corridor, Sri Lanka's Hambantota port, Hungary's Budapest-Belgrade railway, Kazakhstan's Khorgos Gateway, etc. The document on Vision and actions on jointly building Belt and Road itself is alluring for many developing and underdeveloped countries which lack infrastructure. Parama Sinha Palit in her book titled '*Analysing China's Soft Strategy and Comparative Indian Initiatives*' mentions multiple concerns related to these projects[6] such as increasing indebtedness to China, displacement of local workers, emphasis only on extracting resources and less attention to the betterment of the host country which creates doubts about China's intentions. However, one needs to accept that host countries are ready for negotiations over differences. They are not over-rightly renouncing these projects.

Education, Confucius institutes (CI's), the Chinese Diaspora and Tourism play an important role in disseminating Chinese culture and language at the global level. There is an increase in the number of overseas students taking education in China. The Silk Road Belt and Road Initiative scholarship was launched to pursue graduation, post-graduation and Ph.D. degrees from China. The Chinese government has introduced a foundation program which indirectly promotes the Chinese language. CIs conduct

Chinese language courses, and cooking and calligraphy classes. Students prefer to join CIs because they realise that being well versed in the Chinese language will offer them employment opportunities. Recently, there were instances of CI closures. They are pursued as a state propaganda tool but closures do not necessarily reduce the interest to learn the Chinese language. The Chinese Diaspora has to a great extent helped in spreading Chinese cuisine and Chinese medicines. The Chinese who have left their country to uplift themselves from poverty have contributed to the popularity of Chinese food. They have either established Chinese restaurants or worked in restaurants of the host country. Tourism is also promulgating Chinese culture and language. The Chinese language plus tourism courses are becoming popular in various countries.

Chinese '*economic statecraft*'—trade and investment and cultural diplomacy together have helped China in shaping global politics to some extent.[7] In 2013, Sydney University called of the Dalai Lama's visit in order to retain good relations with China, including China's funding for its CI. In 2018, an Australian university had taken disciplinary action against a 20-year-old Philosophy student who supported Hong Kong students' protests. Australia's Deputy Prime Minister underscored the significance of the Chinese market to Australian farmers and expansion of FTA. China was accused of cyber attacks on the federal parliament. However, owing to the positive impact of the China-Australia FTA on Australian farmers, it could not invite displeasure from China. The relation between Australia and China got strained during pandemic as Australia demanded a probe into the origin of the corona virus. Amidst all this, Australian billionaire Andrew Twigyy Forrest invited a Chinese diplomat to the government's press conference by blindsiding health minister Greg Hunt. The Chinese diplomat underlined the responsive and transparent manner of the Chinese government in revealing COVID-19 information.

Cambodia, a receiver of China's aid, has supported China's interests in the South China Sea (SCS). It has assisted China in impeding ASEAN'S consensus against China so that disputes can be managed bilaterally. In 2012, the chairmanship of ASEAN came to Cambodia. For the first time in the history of ASEAN, a joint official statement was not released.

Cambodian delegates had discussed with their Chinese counterparts the wording of the joint communique and opposed the mentioning of the SCS dispute. Similarly in 2016, Cambodia had prevented an international tribunal ruling which criticised China's stand on the SCS. It has also exhibited ASEAN's weakness as a coherent body to deal with the SCS dispute.

On the basis of above discussion, one can derive two findings. First, China perceives its soft power notion of creating a convergence of its own national interests with that of others. But here the question is whether client-countries recognise the Chinese notion of soft power of convergence of national interests. It has been observed that countries like Bangladesh, Sri Lanka and the Maldives prefer to avoid taking sides. Hence, they take advantage of aid provided by any country whether it is China or India or Japan. According to Nilanthi Samaranayake, a director of Policy and Strategy Analysis Program at CNA, 'South Asian countries generally view China as a fall back option and not necessarily a partner of first choice'.[8] She has also observed that these countries are interacting with China and learning from each other's experiences. In the case of Southeast Asia (SEA) and particularly, in the context of the US-China trade war, it can be contended that SEA does not want to choose between China and the USA. During the Shangri-La Dialogue in May 2019, Singapore's Prime Minister Lee Hsien Loong advocated reconciliation between the two and he also urged not to create such conditions which would force other countries to choose between them.[9]

Second, China's notion of soft power has complemented its geo-strategy. As experts have pointed out, China's trade agreements with client-countries and infrastructure development in developing and under-developed countries will secure its geo-strategic interests such as its ever-increasing energy needs, an alternative route to the Strait of Malacca, access to the Indian Ocean, a grip over the South China dispute and the growth of its impoverished Western province—Xinjiang.

China ranks 27th in the 2019 soft power 30 index.[10] Despite pouring in large sums of money in trade, investments and culture, China has not obtained sufficient success in its soft power. Joseph Nye has pointed out two factors limiting China's soft power. First is nationalism. The legitimacy of the Communist Party of China based on economic growth and an appeal to nationalism. It has reduced the global appeal for China. For example, China's activities in the SCS and elsewhere have invited disfavour from its neighbours. The second factor is the hesitance to use civil society and the private sector in spreading soft power. It just relies on the government as a source of soft power. David Shambaugh in an article titled '*China's Soft Power Push: The Search for respect*' has aptly observed the role of the Chinese government in executing soft power tools. According to him, the Chinese communist system has believed that information must be controlled and people must be indoctrinated. In China, propaganda is not a negative term. On the contrary, it is maintained that as China has liberalised its economy the state has to strengthen its hold over information.[11]

Han, C. and Tong, Y. in their article titled '*Students at the Nexus between the Chinese Diaspora and Internationalization of Higher Education: The Role of Overseas Students in China's Strategy of Soft Power*' have illustrated how the Chinese government exerts control over information with the help of 'Ideological and Political Education' (IPE). Chinese students go through compulsory IPE. They are indoctrinated to love the country, the Party, and Socialism. In IPE, textbook 'patriotism' is referred to as the Chinese nation with a Chinese identity and in the same textbook the creation of the PRC under the CCP is considered the end of colonialism. Further, the textbook focuses on the need to endorse national dignity outside China. So, some scholars have noted that when students from the East go West, they are influenced by Western values and ideas. However, in the case of China, it is China which gets the benefits from internationalisation of education because Chinese overseas students defend China's interests.[12] To summarise, China's soft power resources—trade, investment and culture are controlled by the government. There are transparency issues involved. As a result, China's credibility remains low. It is a major hurdle in spreading China's influence.

NOTES

1. Foundation of Alliance Francaise. (2021, January 7). 'Operation of the Foundation.' Retrieved from https://www.fondation-alliancefr.org/?cat=536, accessed on 12 August 2021.
2. Goethe Institute (n.d.). 'Locations.' Retrieved from https://www.goethe.de/en/wwt.html, accessed on 12 August 2021.
3. Deng, Y. (2009). 'The New Hard Realities: "Soft Power and China in Transition"', In M. Li (ed.). *Soft Power: China's Emerging Strategy in International Politics.* Lexington Books. p. 65.
4. Ibid.
5. The State Council The People's Republic of China. (2011, September 6). 'China's Peaceful Development.' Retrieved from http://english.www.gov.cn/archive/white_paper/2014/09/09/content_281474986284646.htm, accessed on 15 June 2017.
6. Palit, P. S. (2017). *Analysing China's Soft Strategy and Comparative Indian Initiatives.* Sage Publications India Pvt. Ltd.
7. Wong, A. (2020, May 22). 'Trading for Influence.' Centre for Strategic and International Studies. Retrieved from https://www.csis.org/analysis/trading-influence, accessed on 21 March 2021.
8. Samaranayake, N. (2019). 'China's Engagement with Smaller South Asian Countries.' (Report No. 446). United States Institute of Peace. Retrieved from https://www.usip.org/sites/default/files/2019-04/sr_446-chinas_engagement_with_smaller_south_asian_countries.pdf, accessed on 1 June 2021.
9. 'PM Lee Hsien Loong's Speech at the 2019 Shangri La Dialogue.' (2019, May 31). *CNA*. Retrieved from https://www.channelnewsasia.com/singapore/lee-hsien-loong-speech-2019-shangri-la-dialogue-882451, accessed on 13 August 2021.
10. 'The Soft Power 30' (n.d.). Retrieved from https://softpower30.com/country/china/ , accessed on 21 March 2021.
11. Shambaugh, D. (2015). 'China's Soft Power Push: The Search for Respect.' *Foreign Affairs,* 94 (4), pp. 99-107. Retrieved from https://www.jstor.org/stable/24483821, accessed on 22 March 2021.
12. Han, C. & Tong, Y. (2021). 'Students at the Nexus between the Chinese Diaspora and Internationalization of Higher Education: The Role of Overseas Students in China's Strategy of Soft Power.' *British Journal of Educational Studies,* pp. 1-20. Retrieved from https://www.tandfonline.com/doi/epub/10.1080/00071005.2021.1935446?needAccess=true, accessed on 7 August 2021.

Bibliography

Abi-Habib, M. (2018, June 25). 'How China Got Sri Lanka to Cough Up the Port', *The New York Times*. Retrieved from https://www.nytimes.com/2018/06/25/world/asia/china-sri-lanka-port.html, accessed on 26 August 2020.

Academy for Cultural Diplomacy. (n.d.). 'Chinese Diaspora'. Retrieved from https://www.culturaldiplomacy.org/academy/index.php?chinese-diaspora, accessed on 24 October 2020.

Ahmed, R. (2018, May 18). 'Free Trade Agreement with China: A Necessity.' *Dhaka Tribune*. https://www.dhakatribune.com/opinion/op-ed/2018/05/18/free-trade-agreement-with-china-a-necessity, accessed on 4 August 2019.

Aires, B. (2018, May 7). 'Interview: Confucius Institutes Bridge LatAm, Chinese Cultures.' *Xinhua Net*. Retrieved from http://www.xinhuanet.com/english/2018-05/07/c_137161363.htm, accessed on 5 November 2020.

Aliyev, N. (2019, December 19). 'China's Soft Power in Central Asia. The Central Asia Caucasus,' *ANALYST,*. Retrieved from https://www.caci analyst.org/publications/analytical-articles/item/13599-chinas-soft-power-in-central-asia.html, accessed on 23 October 2020.

An, W. X. (2019). 'China's Evolving Policy towards the Chinese Diaspora in Southeast Asia (1949-2018*).*' *ISEAS Yusof Ishak Institute* (14), pp. 1-25. Retrieved from https://eresources.nlb.gov.sg/printheritage/detail/2ed87b51-1fe2-44b0-876b-1a46fc4accea.aspx, accessed on 22 October 2020.

'Annual Outflow of Foreign Direct Investment (FDI) from China between 2010 and 2020'. (n.d.). *Statista*. Retrieved from https://www.statista.com/

statistics/858019/china-outward-foreign-direct-investment-flows/, accessed on 15 0ctober 2020.

Arshad, M. U. & Haidong, Z. (2017). 'China-Pakistan Economic Corridor (CPEC), Issues/Barrier and Imperatives of Pakistan and China. *International Interdisciplinary Business-Economics Advancement Journal,* 2(2), pp. 104-114. Retrieved from DOI: 10.5038/2640-6489.2.2.1023, accessed on 21 August 2020.

Ba, A. D. (2003). 'China and ASEAN: Re-navigating Relations for 21st Century Asia. *Asian Survey,* 43 (4), pp. 622-647. Retrieved from https://www.jstor.org/stable/10.1525/as.2003.43.4.622, accessed on 22 March 2021.

Bachrach, P. & Baratz, M. S. (1963). 'Decisions and Non decisions: An Analytical Framework.' *The American Political Science Review,* 57(3), pp. 632-642. Retrieved from https://www.jstor.org/stable/1952568, accessed on February 13, 2017.

Balachandran, P. K. (2019, February 8). 'Fate of Maldives-China FTA Uncertain as Male Loosens Ties with Beijing' bilateral.org,. Retrieved from https://www.bilaterals.org/?fate-of-maldives-china-fta, accessed on 15 November 2020.

Balchandran, P.K. (2018, May 24). 'China Vigorously Uses Educational Facilities as Instruments of Soft Power.' *The Citizen.* Retrieved from https://www.thecitizen.in/index.php/en/NewsDetail/index/5/13865/Chinas-VigorOf-Educational-Facilities-As-Instruments-Of-Soft-Power, accessed on 22 October 2020.

Baldwin, D. A. (2013). 'Power and International Relations.' In W. Carlsnaes, T. Risse & Beth. A. Simmons (eds.), *Handbook of International Relations,* London: Sage Publications Ltd.

'Bangladesh's Geopolotical Importance 'Grows'.(2017, May 29). *The Independent.* Retrieved from https://m.theindependentbd.com/printversion/details/96789 accessed 4 April 2020.

'Belt and Road Forum for International Cooperation'. (2017, April 10). *Vision and Actions on Jointly Building Belt and Road.* Retrieved from http://beltandroadforum.org/english/n100/2017/0410/c22-45-4.html accessed on 3 April 2020.

Bernhard, N. (n.d.). '*President Harry Truman Enlisted Journalists in Cold War: Are there Parallels Between then and now?* Nieman Reports. Retrieved from https://niemanreports.org/articles/president-harry-truman-enlisted-journalists-in-the-cold-war/, accessed on 2 June 2021.

Bhattacharjee, J). 2018, June 27). '*Decoding China-Bangladesh Relatioship*'. Observer Research Foundation. Retrieved from https://www.orfonline.org/expert-speak/41935-decoding-china-bangladesh-relationship/?amp, accessed on 5 April 2020.

Bitabarova, A. (2018). 'Unpacking Sino-Central Asian Engagement along the New Silk Road: A Case Study of Kazakhstan'. *Journal of Contemporary East Asia*, 7 (2), pp. 149-173. Retrieved from https://www.tandfonline.com/doi/full/10.1080/24761028.2018.1553226, accessed on 1 December 2020.

Breslin, S. (2011). *The Soft Notion of China's 'Soft Power*. London: Chatham House, pp. 1-18. Retrieved from https://www.chathamhouse.org/sites/default/files/public/Research/Asia/0211pp_breslin.pdf, accessed on 13 May 2016.

Cabinet Office of the Prime Minister. (2017, June 1). 'Hungary is an Ideal Pillar of the One Belt, One Road. Retrieved from https://miniszterelnok.hu/hungary-is-an-ideal-pillar-of-the-one-belt-one-road-initiative/, accessed on 10 October 2020.

Centre For Language Education And Cooperatio. (2021, February 2). '*China Becomes the Official Language of United Nations World Tourism Organization, and the Development of "Chinese+Goes" Further,*' retrieved from http://www.chinese.cn/page/#/pcpage/article?id=499 accessed on 28 February 2021.

CGTN. (2019, June 14). '*Tajikistan on 'Belt and Road' to further prosperity,*' retrieved from https://news.cgtn.com/news/2019-06-14/Tajikistan-on-Belt-and-Road-to-further-prosperity-HvKdOh1nfW/index.html, accessed on 27 November 2020.

Chan, W. T. (1969). *A Source Book in Chinese Philosophy*. New Jersey: Princeton University Press.

Chatterjee, A. (2020), 'Sri Lanka & the Belt and Road Initiative: A Balancing Act in the Indian Ocean Region.' *Defence and Security Journal*, 5, pp. 47-56. Retrieved from https://calhoun.nps.edu/bitstream/handle/10945/66470/Chatterjee-article%20%281%29.pdf?sequence=1&isAllowed=y, accessed on 15 July 2021.

Chaudhury, D. R. (2021, July 26). 'Myanmar's Military Junta Revives Scope of BRI Projects'. *The Economic Times*. Retrieved from https://economictimes.indiatimes.com/news/international/world-news/

myanmars-military-junta-revives-scope-of-bri-projects/articleshow/84739776.cms?from=mdr, accessed on 7 August 2021.

Chazan, Y. (2020, January 24). 'China BRI Ventures Run into Trouble in Kazakhstan'. *Asia Sentinel.* Retrieved from https://www.asiasentinel.com/p/china-bri-ventures-run-into-trouble, accessed on 2 December 2020.

China Education Centre. (n.d). *Complete Guide to China Scholarships: Two Approaches to Study in China on Scholarship.* Retrieved from https://www.chinaeducenter.com/en/cedu/ceduproject211.php, accessed on 15 November 2020.

'China Forges Agreement with 54 Countries on Mutual Recognition of Higher Education Degrees. (2020, Spetember 5). *Xinhua Net, r*Retrieved from http://www.xinhuanet.com/english/2020-09/05/c_139345581.htm, accessed on 22 November 2020.

'China Joins Treaty of Amity, Cooperation in Southeast Asia. (2003, October 9). *People's Daily Online.* Retrieved from: http://en.people.cn/200310/08/eng20031008_125556.shtml, accessed on 2 August 2019.

China Power. (n.d.). *Is China Attracting Foreign Visitors* retrieved from https://chinapower.csis.org/tourism/, accessed on 16 November 2020.

China Scholar. (n.d.). '*China Belt and Road Scholarship*' retrieved from https://www.china-scholar.com/scholarships/belt-and-road-initiative-scholarships-bri,/ accessed on 15 October 2020.

China Tourism Academy (Data Centre for Ministry of Culture and Tourism). Retrieved from http://eng.ctaweb.org.cn/, accessed on 18 November 2020.

Chow, G. C. (2015). *China's economic transformation.* UK: John Wiley & Sons. Ltd.

Chow, G. C. (2018). 'China's Economic Transformation.' In R. Garnaut, L. Song & C. Fang (eds.). *China's 40 Years of Reforms and Development 1978-2018*, Australian National University Press.

Clarke, M. (2017). 'The Belt and Road Initiative: China's New Grand Strategy?' *Asia Policy*, (24*)*, pp. 71-79. Retrieved from https://www.jstor.org/stable/26403204, accessed on 22 September 2020.

'CPEC Not Benefitting People of Balochistan: Provincial Minister'. (2021, February 6). *ANI.* Retrieved from https://www.aninews.in/news/world/asia/cpec-not-benefitting-people-of-balochistan-provincial-minister20210206160425/, accessed on 9 June 2021.

Dahl, R. A. (1957). 'The Concept of Power'. *Behavioural Science*, 2 (3), 201-

215. Retrieved from https://welcometorel.files.wordpress.com/2008/08/conceptpower_r-dahl.pdf, accessed on May 16, 2017.

Damuri, Y. R.; Perkasa, V.; Atje, R.; & Hirawan, F. (2019). '*Perceptions and Readiness of Indonesia Towards The Belt and Road Initiative*'. Indonesia: Centre for Strategic and International Studies. Retrieved from https://www.csis.or.id/uploads/attachments/post/2019/05/23/CSIS_BRI_Indonesia_r.pdf, accessed on 15 April 2020.

Deng, Y. (2009). 'The New Hard Realities: Soft Power and China in Transition', in M. Li (ed.), *Soft Power: China's Emerging Strategy in International Politics.* Lexington Books.

Ding, S. (2014, April). 'Chinese Soft Power and Public Diplomacy: An Analysis of China's New Diaspora Engagement policies in Xi Era', *East Asia Institute.*,retrieved from http://www.eai.or.kr/data/bbs/eng_report/201404011627122.pdf, accessed on 22 October 2020.

Dunne, T. & Schmidt, B. C. (2008). 'Realism'. In J. Baylis, S. Smith, & P. Owens P. (eds.). *The Globalization of World Politics: An Introduction to International Relations.* New York: Oxford University Press.

Eastern Opening. (2018, May 21). The Orange Files. Retrieved from https://theorangefiles.hu/eastern-opening/, accessed on 9 October 2020.

Ebrahimian, B. A. and Dorfman, Z. (2019, May 14). 'China has been Running Global Influence Campaigns for Years,' *The Atlantic*, https://www.theatlantic.com/international/archive/2019/05/beijing-olympics-china-influence-campaigns/589186/, accessed on 20 November 2020.

Eno, R. (2015). *The Analects of Confucius—The Online Teaching Translation.* Retrieved from https://chinatxt.sitehost.iu.edu/Analects_of_Confucius_(Eno-2015).pdf, accessed on 20 August 2021.

Esteban, M. (2016). China-Pakistan Corridor: A Transit, Economic or Development Corrior. *Strategic Studies*, 36 (2), pp. 63-74. Retrieved from https://www.jstor.org/stable/48535947, accessed on 25 July 2020.

Fang, C. (2010). 'Labour Market Development and Expansion of Rural and Urban Employment'. In C. Fang (ed.). *Transforming the Chinese Economy.* Netherlands: Koninklijke Brill NV.

Fang, X. (2015).'The Belt and Road Initiative: Connecting China and Central Europe. *International Issues and Slovac Foreign Policy Affairs*, 24(3), pp. 3-14. Retrieved from https://www.jstor.org/stable/26591865?seq=11#metadata_info_tab_contents, accessed on 1 August 2020.

Farr, G. (2017, July 10). 'Pakistan's Role In China's One Belt One Road

Initiative'. *e-International Relations,* https://www.e-ir.info/2017/07/10/pakistans-role-in-chinas-one-belt-one-road-initiative/, accessed on 7 June 2021.

Fenby, J. (2013). *The Penguin History of Modern China: The Fall and Rise of a Great Power, 1850 to the Present.* England: Penguin Books.

Feng, D. (2021, April 19). 'BRI, a Cornerstone for Growth in Pakistan. *Global Times.* Retrieved from https://www.globaltimes.cn/page/202104/1221462.shtml, accessed on 30 June 2021.

Foundation of Alliance Francaise. (2021, January 7). '*Operation of the Foundation.*' Retrieved from https://www.fondation-alliancefr.org/?cat=536, accessed on 12 August 2021.

French, H. W. (2006, April 1) '.Another Chinese Export Is All the Rage: China's Language.' *The New York Times.* Retrieved from https://www.nytimes.com/2006/01/11/world/asia/another-chinese-export-is-all-the-rage-chinas-language.html, accessed on 2 November 2020.

French, H. W. (2014). *China's second continent: How a million migrants are building a new empire in Africa.* New York: Vintage Books.

Gibbs, S. (2019, October 15). *Mandarin Classes in Venezuela on the Rise.* CGTN America. Retrieved from https://america.cgtn.com/2019/10/13/mandarin-classes-in-venezuela-on-the-rise, accessed on 5 November 2020.

Gill, B. & Huang, Y. (2006). 'Sources and limits of Chinese 'Soft Power'. *Survival, 48*(2), pp. 17-36. Retrieved from https://www.comw.org/cmp/fulltext/0606gill.pdf, accessed on 25 March 2016.

Gittings, J. (2005). *The Changing Face of China from Mao to Market.* New York: Oxford University Press.

Goethe Institute (n.d.). *Locations.* Retrieved from https://www.goethe.de/en/wwt.html, accessed on 12 August 2021.

Grossman, D. (2020, June 11). 'What China Wants in South Asia.' Observer Research Foundation, (368). Retrieved from https://www.orfonline.org/research/what-china-wants-in-south-asia-67665/, accessed on 19 September2020.

Hajari, N. (2018, November 2). 'Who Should be Afraid of One Belt One Road? China.' *The Print.* Retrieved from https://theprint.in/defence/who-should-be-afraid-of-one-belt-one-road-china/144136/, accessed on 3 August 2020.

Han, C. & Tong, Y. (2021). 'Students at the Nexus between the Chinese Diaspora and Internationalization of Higher Education: The Role of

Overseas Students in China's Strategy of Soft Power', *British Journal of Educational Studies,* pp. 1-20. Retrieved from https://www.tandfonline.com/doi/epub/10.1080/00071005.2021.1935446?needAccess=true, accessed on 7 August 2021.

He, L. W. (2019, April 12). 'How China is Closing the Soft Power Gap in Latin America.' *Americas Quarterly,*.retrieved from https://www.americasquarterly.org/article/how-china-is-closing-the-soft-power-gap-in-latin-america,/ accessed on 24 October 2020.

'Hu Urges Enhamcing Soft Power of Chinese Culture.' (2007, October 15). *China Daily.* Retrieved from https://www.chinadaily.com.cn/china/2007-10/15/content_6226620.htm, accessed on 5 November 2020.

Huang, Y. & Ding, S. (2006). 'Dragon's underbelly: An analysis of China's soft power.' *East Asia,* 23(4), pp. 22-44. Retrieved from DOI:10.1007/BF03179658, accessed on 25 April 2016.

Hundlani, D. & Kannangara, P. (2020, May 7). 'The Belt and Road in Sri Lanka: Beyond the Debt Trap Discussion' *The Diplomat.* Retrieved from https://thediplomat.com/2020/05/the-belt-and-road-in-sri-lanka-beyond-the-debt-trap-discussion/, accessed on 24 June 2021.

International Trade Administration. (2021, February 3). 'China-Country Commercial Guide' retrieved from https://www.trade.gov/knowledge-product/china-trade-agreements#:~:text=China%20maintains%2016%20Free %20Trade,implementing%20an%20additional%20eight%20FTAs, accessed on 12 April 2021.

Jacques, M. (2008, June 11). 'As China's Power Grows the Diaspora Starta to Flex its Worlwide Muscle. *The Guardian.* Retrieved from https://www.theguardian.com/commentisfree/2008/jun/11/china.comment, accessed on 23 October 2020.

Jacques, M. (2009). *When China rules the world: the end of the western world and the birth of global order.* New York: The Penguin Press.

Jain, R. (2018). 'China's Economic Expansion in South Asia: Strengths, Challenges and opportunies. *International Journal of Asian Affairs,* 31 (1/2), pp. 21-36. Retrieved from https://www.jstor.org/stable/26608821, accessed on 20 August 2020.

Jakhar, P. (2019, September 6). *Confucius Institutes: The Growth of China's Controvercial Cultural Branch, BBC News.* retrieved from https://www.bbc.com/news/amp/world-asia-china-49511231, accessed on 22 October 2020.

Joseph, W. A. (2014). 'Ideology and China's Political Development.' In W. A. Joseph (ed.). *Politics in China an Introduction*. New York: Oxford University Press.

Kang, H. (n.d.). *Reframing Cultural Diplomacy*: International Cultural Politics of Soft Power and the Creative Economy. Retrieved from https://www.culturaldiplomacy.org/academy/content/pdf/participant-papers/2011-08-loam/Reframing-Cultural-Diplomacy-International-Cultural-Politics-of-Soft-Power-and-the-Creative-Economy-Hyungseok-Kang.pdf, accessed on 25 October 2020.

Kayani. F.N.; Ahmed,M.; Shah, T.A.; & Kayani, U.N. (2013). 'China-Pakistan Economic Relations: Lessons for Pakistan'. *Journal of Commerce and Social Sciences*, vol. 7(3), 454-462. retrieved from https://papers.ssrn.com/sol3/papers.cfm?abstract_id=2892052, accessed on 2 April 2020.

Kemenade, W. V. (2008). *Détente Between China and India: The Delicate Balance of Geopolitics in Asia*, pp. 1-230, Netherlands Institute of International Relations, Clingendael. Retrieved from https://www.clingendael.org/sites/default/files/pdfs/20080700_cdsp_diplomacy_paper.pdf, accessed on 29 March 2020.

Khan, M. Z. (2016, July 6). 'Pakistan, China Yet to Strike Deal on FTA Phase-II. *Dawn*. Retrieved from https://www.dawn.com/news/1269281, accessed on 10 September 2020.

Kondapalli, S. (2014, November 13). *Maritime Silk Road:Increasing Chinese Inroads into Maldives*. Institute of Peace and Conflict Studies. Retrieved from http://www.ipcs.org/comm_select.php?articleNo=4735, accessed on 14 November 2020.

Koutantou, A. (2021, May 28). *China's COSCO Hopes for Greek Deal on Piraeus Despite Delay-Official. Reuters*. Retrieved from https://www.reuters.com/article/us-cosco-ship-hold-greece-piraeus-idUSKCN2D91H7, accessed on 15 July 2021.

Krishnan, A. (2020, August 9). 'What are Confucius Institutes, and why are they under the scanner in India.' *The Hindu*. retrieved from https://www.thehindu.com/news/national/the-hindu-explains-what-are-confucius-institutes-and-why-are-they-under-the-scanner-in-india/article32306693.ece, accessed on 15 November 2020.

Kuo, M. (2020, November 23). 'Malaysia in China's Belt and Road: Insights From Chow Bing Ngeow.' *The Diplomat*. Retrieved from https://thediplomat.com/2020/11/malaysia-in-chinas-belt-and-road/, accessed on 8 June

'Interview China, ASEAN Trade Economic Cooperation to Make New Start.' retrieved from http://fta.mofcom.gov.cn/enarticle/enasean/chianaseannews/201411/18854_1.html, accessed on 5 August 2019.

Ministry of Commerce, People's Republic of China. (2019, April 11). 'The 11th Meeting of the 2nd Phase of Negotiation of China-Pakistan FTA Makes Positive Progress' retrieved from http://fta.mofcom.gov.cn/enarticle/enpakistan/enpakistannews/201904/40278_1.html, accessed on 4 April 2020.

Ministry of Commerce, People's Republic of China. (2017, December 8). 'China and Maldives Sign the Free Trade Agreement,' retrieved from http://fta.mofcom.gov.cn/enarticle/chinamedfen/chinamedfennews/201712/36458_1.html, accessed on 15 Novenber 2020.

Ministry of Commerce, People's Republic of China. (2009, August 19). 'ASEAN- China FTA Investment Agreement Signed.' retrieved from http://fta.mofcom.gov.cn/enarticle/enasean/chianaseannews/200911/1473_1.html, accessed on 4 August 2019.

Ministry of Education, People's Republic of China. (2009, March 13). 'Circular of the Ministry of Education on Undergraduate Foundation Program for International Students on the Chinese Government Scholarship Program'. Retrieved from http://en.moe.gov.cn/documents/laws_policies/201506/t20150626_191403.html, accessed on 20 November 2020.

Ministry of Education, The People's Republic of China. (2019, April 18). '*Statistical Report on International Students in China for 2018*',rRetrieved from http://en.moe.gov.cn/documents/reports/201904/t20190418_378692.html, accessed on 20 November 2020.

Ministry of Foreign Affairs of the People's Republic of China. (2015, March 28). 'Vision and Actions on Jointly Building Silk Road Economic Belt and 21st-Century Maritime Silk Road'. Retrieved from https://www.fmprc.gov.cn/mfa_eng/zxxx_662805/t1249618.shtml, accessed on 1 August 2020.

Mohanty, M. (2014). *Ideology Matters: China From Mao Zedong to Xi Jinping.* Delhi: Aakar Books.

Morgenthau, H. J. (1948). *Politics among Nations: The Struggle for Power and Peace.* New York: Alfred A. Knopf.

'Myanmar Junta Implementing China's BRI Projects by Stealth.' (2021, July 23). *The Irrawaddy.* Retrieved from https://www.irrawaddy.com/opinion/analysis/myanmar-junta-implementing-chinas-bri-projects-by-stealth.html, accessed on 7 August 2021.

Nye Jr, J. S. (1990). 'The Changing Nature of World Power.' *Political Science Quarterly,* 105(2), pp. 177-192. Retrieved from https://www.jstor.org/stable/2151022, accessed on 20 February 2017.

Nye Jr, J. S. (1990). 'Soft Power.' *Foreign Policy,* 80, pp. 153-171. Retrieved from https://www.jstor.org/stable/1148580, accessed on 17 January 2017.

Nye Jr, J.S. (1990). *Bound to Lead: The Changing Nature of American Power.* Basic Books.

Nye Jr, J. S. (2002). *The Paradox of American Power: Why the World's Only Super Power Can't Go it Alone.* Oxford University Press.

Nye Jr, J. S. (2008). 'Public Diplomacy and Soft Power.' *Annals of the American Academy of Political and Social Science,* 616, pp. 94-109. Retrieved from https://www.jstor.org/stable/25097996, accessed on 20 February 2017.

Nye Jr, J. S. (2012, May 8). 'China's Soft Power Deficit.' *WSJ.* Retrieved from https://www.wsj.com/articles/SB10001424052702304451104577389923098678842, accessed on 25 March 2016.

Nye Jr, J. S. (2009). 'Get Smart: Combining Hard and Soft Power.' *Foreign Policy,* 88(4), pp. 160-163. Retrieved from https://www.jstor.org/stable/20699631, accessed on 17 September 2015.

Nye Jr, J. S. (2012). *Soft Power: The Means to Success in World Politics.* New Delhi: KW Publishers Pvt. Ltd.

Ohashi, H. (2005). 'China's Regional Trade and Investment Prolific.' In D. Shambaugh (ed.). *Power shift China and Asia's New Dynamics.* California: University of California.

Overholt, W. H. (1993). *The rise of China: How economic reform is creating a new superpower.* New York: WW Norton & Company.

Palit, P. S. (2017). *Analysing China's Soft Power Strategy and Comparative Indian Initiatives.* New Delhi: Sage Publications India Pvt. Ltd.

Parameswaran, P. (2019, April 23). 'Malaysia's Evolving Approach to China's Belt and Road Initiative.' *The Diplomat* retrieved from https://thediplomat.com/2019/04/malaysias-evolving-approach-to-chinas-belt-and-road-initiative,/ accessed on 21 July 2020.

Parameswaran, P. (2019, July 9). 'Where is Indonesia on China's Belt and Road Initiative?' *The Diplomat.* Retrieved from https://thediplomat.com/2019/07/where-is-indonesia-on-chinas-belt-and-road-initiative/, accessed on 15 October 2020.

'Perceptions of China's Belt and Road Initiative and Investments in Sri Lanka.'

(2021, April 6). *Daily FT*. Retrieved from https://www.ft.lk/front-page/Perceptions-of-China-s-Belt-Road-Initiative-and-investments-in-Sri-Lanka/44-715870, accessed on 24 June 2021.

PM Lee Hsien Loong's Speech at the 2019 Shangri La Dialogue. (2019, May 31). CNA. Retrieved from https://www.channelnewsasia.com/singapore/lee-hsien-loong-speech-2019-shangri-la-dialogue-882451, accessed on 13 August 2021.

Prathibha, M. S. (2017). 'China-Pakistan Economic Corridor'. In S. Kondapalli & H. Xiaowen (eds.) *One Belt One Road: China's Global Outreach*. New Delhi: Pentagon Press.

Press Trust of India. (2018, June 26). 'China's Acquisition of Sri Lankan Hambantota Port Highlights 'Debt Trap' to gain influence around World, Says Report'. *Firstpost*. retrieved from https://www.firstpost.com/world/chinas-acquisition-of-sri-lankan-hambantota-port-highlights-debt-trap-to-gain-influence-around-world-says-report-4599911.html, accessed on 24 March 2021.

Procopio, M. (2015, July). 'The Effectiveness of Confucius Institutes as a Tool of China's Soft Power in South Africa.' *African East-Asian Affairs*, (2), pp. 98-125 retrieved from https://www.researchgate.net/publication/282840886_The_effectiveness_of_Confucius_Institutes_as_a_tool_of_China's_soft_power_in_South_Africa, accessed on 23 October 2020.

Przychodniak, M. (2019, May 8). 'Confucius Institutes: A Tool For Promoting China's Interests.' *CHOICE*. Retrieved from https://chinaobservers.eu/confucius-institutes-as-a-tool-for-promoting-chinas-interests/, accessed on 20 October 2020.

Putri, R., & Jeevan, J. (2018). 'The Implications of One Belt One Road (OBOR) Strategy on Malaysian Seaport Capacity.' *Advances in Transportation and Logistics Reseach*, 1, pp. 652-667. Retrieved from https://proceedings.itltrisakti.ac.id/index.php/ATLR/article/view/70, accessed on 20 July 2020.

Saili, L.; Lee, V.; & Lin, Z. (eds.). (2013). *China's External Economic Relations*. Singapore: Enrich Professional Publishing.

Samaranayake, N. (2019). '*China's Engagement with Smaller South Asian Countries*. (Report No. 446). United States Institute of Peace. Retrieved from https://www.usip.org/sites/default/files/2019-04/sr_446-chinas_engagement_with_smaller_south_asian_countries.pdf, accessed on 1 June 2021.

Samaranayake, N. (2021, March 2). 'Chinese Belt and Road Investment is not all Bad or Good.' *Foreign Policy*. Retrieved from https://foreignpolicy.com/2021/03/02/sri-lanka-china-bri-investment-debt-trap/, accessed on 24 June 2021.

Saran, S. (2015, October 9). 'What China's One Belt and Road Strategy Means for India, Asia and the World.' *The Wire*. Retrieved from https://thewire.in/external-affairs/what-chinas-one-belt-and-one-road-strategy-means-for-india-asia-and-the-world, accessed on 15 July 2020.

Sareen, S. (2019, February 20). 'For Pakistan, China is the New America.' Observer Research Foundation. https://www.orfonline.org/expert-speak/pakistan-china-new-america-48305/, accessed on 10 December 2019.

Sayeed, K. B. (1964). 'Pakistan's Foreign Policy: An Analysis of Pakistani Fears and Interests.' *Asian Survey*, 4(3), 746-756. Retrieved from https://www.jstor.org/stable/302356, accessed on 29 March 2020.

Shambaugh, D. (ed.). (2006). *Power Shift: China and Asia's New Dynamics*. Berkeley, Los Angeles, London: University of California Press.

Shambaugh, D. (2015). 'China's Soft Power Push: The Search for respect.' *Foreign Affairs,* 94 (4), pp. 99-107. Retrieved from https://www.jstor.org/stable/24483821, accessed on 22 March 2021.

Shapiro, J. (2017, January 12). 'One Belt, One Road, No Dice'. *Geopolitical Futures,* r Retrieved from https://geopoliticalfutures.com/one-belt-one-road-no-dice, accessed on 2 August 2020.

Sharma, S. D. (2009). *China and India in the age of globalisation*. New Delhi: Cambridge University Press.

Sibal, S. (2019, December 14). 'Maldives–China FTA ID Dead, CAB India's Internal Matter: Speaker of the Maldives Parliament.' *DNA*. Retrieved from https://www.dnaindia.com/india/report-maldives-china-fta-is-dead-cab-india-s-internal-matter-speaker-of-the-maldives-parliament-2805478, accessed on 15 November 2020.

Siddiqui, M. S. (2019, March 15). 'China-Bangladesh FTA: An Overview.' *The Financial Express*. Retrieved from https://thefinancialexpress.com.bd/views/china-bangladesh-fta-an-overview-, accessed on 15 May 2019.

Slingerland, E. G. (2001). Kongzi (Confucius) 'The Analects'. In P. J. Ivanhoe & B.W. Von Norden (eds.) *Readings in Classical Chinese Philosophy*. Seven Bridges Press. Retrieved from https://www.docdroid.net/aoKoDKB/p-j-ivanhoe-bryan-w-van-norden-readings-in-classical-chinese-philosophy-2000-pdf#page=62, accessed on 23 September 2018.

Smith, J. (2020, October 28). *China and Maldives: Lessons From the Indian Ocean's New Battleground.* The Heritage Foundation. retrieved from https://www.heritage.org/global-politics/report/china-and-the-maldives-lessons-the-indian-oceans-new-battleground, accessed on 15 November 2020.

Sooriyan, A. (2018, August 27). 'The Unofficial Ambassadors: A Comparative Study of Indian and Chinese Diaspora in Southeast Asia.' Chennai Centre for China Studies. Retrieved from https://www.c3sindia.org/culture-history/the-unofficial-ambassadors-a-comparative-study-of-indian-and-chinese-diaspora-in-southeast-asia-by-anusha-sooriyan,/ accessed on 23 October 2020

Standish, R. (2019, October 1). 'China's Path Forward is Getting Bumpy.' *The Atlantic.* Retrieved from https://www.theatlantic.com/international/archive/2019/10/china-belt-road-initiative-problems-kazakhstan/597853, accessed on 27 November 2020.

Tan, H. (2016, August 11). *President Xi Expands China's Soft Power Through Tourism. CNBC.* Retrieved from https://www.cnbc.com/2016/08/10/president-xi-expands-chinas-soft-power-through-tourism.html, accessed on 16 November 2020.

Than, K.& Komuves, A. (2020, April 24). 'Update 3-Hungary, China sign Loan Deal for Budapest-Belgrade Chinese Rail Project.' *Reuters.* retrieved from https://www.reuters.com/article/hungary-china-railway-loan-idUSL5N2CC6A0, accessed on 9 October 2020.

The Soft Power 30 (n. d.). Retrieved from https://softpower30.com/country/china/, accessed on 21 March 2021.

The State Council, The People's Republic of China. (2011, September 6). 'China's Peaceful Development.' Retrieved from http://english.www.gov.cn/archive/white_paper/2014/09/09/content_281474986284646.htm, accessed on 15 June 2017.

The World Factbook. (n.d.). *Pakistan.* Retrieved from https://www.cia.gov/the-world factbook/countries/pakistan/ accessed on 4 April 2020.

Thussu, D.K. (2016). *Communicating India's Soft Power: Buddha to Bollywood.* Sage/Vistaar.

'Timeline: Olympic Torch Protests around the World'. (2008, April 28) *Reuters.* Retrieved from https://www.reuters.com/article/us-olympics-torch-disruptions-idUSSP17070920080428, accessed on 23 October 2020.

Tower, J. & Clapp, P. A. (2021, June 8). 'Myanmar: China, the Coup and the

Future'. United States Institute of Peace. Retrieved from https://www.usip.org/publications/2021/06/myanmar-china-coup-and-future, accessed on 20 July 2021.

Urban, M. (2012, August 13). 'Will Olympics Prove a Bargain for UK Soft Power Gains? *BBC News*. Retrieved from https://www.bbc.com/news/uk-19250118, accessed on 15 March 2021.

Vogel, E. F. (2011). *Deng Xiaoping and the Trasformation of China.* London: The Belknap Press of Harvard University Press.

Wai, C. S. (2017, April 30). 'China's 'One Big Family Policy Raises Concerns.' *The Strait Times*. Retrieved from https://www.straitstimes.com/opinion/chinas-one-big-family-policy-raises-concerns, accessed on 10 November 2020.

'Where Does Burma Stand on China's 'One Belt, One Road?' (2017, May 12). *The Irrawaddy*. retrieved from: https://www.irrawaddy.com/opinion/editorial/burma-stand-chinas-one-belt-one-road.html, accessed on 21 August 2019.

Wong, A. (2020, May 22). 'Trading for Influence.' Centre for Strategic and International Studies. Retrieved from https://www.csis.org/analysis/trading-influence, accessed on 21 March 2021.

Xi, C. (2020, July 5). 'New NGO to Operate China's Confucius Institutes, 'disperse misinterpretation'. *Global Times*. Retrieved from https://www.globaltimes.cn/content/1193584.shtml, accessed on 10 November 2020.

Yergaliyeva, A. (2019, October 24). 'Kazakh Government Estimates NurlyZhol Program will cost $ 16.91 Billion Over Next Five Years.' *The Astana Times*. Retrieved from https://astanatimes.com/2019/10/kazakh-government-estimates-nurly-zhol-programme-will-cost-16-91-billion-over-next-five-years/, accessed on 1 December 2020.

Yhome, K. (2018, July 11). 'The BRI and Myanmar's China Debate'. Observer Research Foundation. Retrieved from https://www.orfonline.org/expert-speak/bri-myanmar-china-debate,/ accessed on 8 June 2021.

Yongmei, Y. (2004, January 7). 'UN report: China becoming major investor abroad.' (Z. Xiaoning, Interviewer). *People's Daily*. Retrieved from http://en.people.cn/200401/07/eng20040107_132003.shtml, accessed on 12 October 2020.

Yu, H. (2017). 'China's Belt and Road Initiative and its Implications for Southeast Asia. *Asia Policy*, (24), pp. 117-122. Retrieved from https://

www.jstor.org/stable/26403210, accessed on 4 August 2019.

Yu, R. (2020, March 29). 'China's Public Diplomacy Strategy in Latin America and Caribbean.' *Sigma Iota Rho Journal of International Relations*. Retrieved from http://www.sirjournal.org/op-ed/2020/3/29/chinas-public-diplomacy-strategy-in-latin-america-and-the-caribbean, accessed on 3 November 2020.

Zhe, R. (2010, June 22). 'Confucius Institutes: China's Soft Power?' *Rising Powers Initiative*. Retrieved from https://www.risingpowersinitiative.org/2010/06/22/confucius-institutes-chinas-soft-power/, accessed on 2 November 2020.

Zhu, X. (2012). 'Understanding China's Growth: Past, Present and Future.' *Journal of Economic Perspective,* Vol. 26, (November 4), pp. 103-124. https://pubs.aeaweb.org/doi/pdfplus/10.1257/jep.26.4.103, accessed on15 April 2019.

Index